HEAL MONEY TR,
SUSTAINABLE WEALTH

Lindsay Lawless is a former Corporate Account turned Money Consciousness Coach who has helped countless women heal their relationship with money. Using her 10+ years of money & financial knowledge as well as her own money transformation story, she helps women to feel confident and powerful through owning their personal & business finances.

HEAL MONEY TRAUMA & CREATE SUSTAINABLE WEALTH

THE NO BS APPROACH TO FINANCIAL ENLIGHTENMENT

LINDSAY LAWLESS

The events and conversations in this book have been set down to the best of the author's ability, although some names and details have been changed to protect the privacy of individuals.

First paperback edition September 2019

Cover design by Alyssa Watson Lee and Lindsay Lawless
Photography and illustrations by Tanner Albright

ISBN 978-1-892324-72-6

www.lawlessbalance.com

For my grandmother Elizabeth King (Meme) whose life long mission of advocacy & community service inspires me every day to have a massive impact in the lives of women everywhere and continue her legacy.

As well as my mother Lysa Lawless, whose guidance, love, and endless support laid the foundation for me to be the best version of myself.

HEAL MONEY TRAUMA & CREATE SUSTAINABLE WEALTH

PART I MONEY MINDSET & WHY IT IS ABOUT SO MUCH MORE

PART III TRANSFORMATIONAL MONEY STORIES FROM EXTRAORDINARY WOMEN LIKE YOU

HEAL MONEY TRAUMA & CREATE SUSTAINABLE WEALTH

INTRODUCTION

Once you experience an awakening, become aware of your thoughts and beliefs, and start making conscious choices to shift the dialogue, you can navigate your way out of debt and financial overwhelm. You can say goodbye to mediocrity, confusion, and scarcity. You can stop living in constant financial struggle and believing the lie that there is no way out or that's just the way it is. As you start to shine a spotlight on your relationship with money and bring your awareness to it, you can begin to heal. You can begin to step into your greatness and harness the power necessary to manifest wealth. The kind of wealth that goes far beyond money. Wealth that is sustainable and allows you to build a legacy for you and your family.

The first step is mastering your mindset. This is the foundation for your entire life, and your finances are no different. As we embark on this journey through the mind, we will dive deeper and explore the emotional and spiritual components that affect your relationships. The relationship with yourself, others and ultimately, how these factors impact your relationship with money. We will gain an understanding of your money story and shift this narrative to one that supports you and your dreams. This is essential to unlocking your infinite potential and aligning with your highest self.

After you've mastered this, we will share success stories from ordinarily extraordinary women just like you and I. Women who have taken control of their lives and finances to rewrite their story, transform their relationship with money, and create sustainable wealth. These women have overcome all of the odds to break generational curses, ditch scarcity, shift their mindset, and heal. So you can see and believe it's possible for you too. To overcome adversity and step into abundance, regardless of your circumstances.

Once you're inspired and ready to take action, we will learn the financial strategies you need to know to take full ownership of your money. This final section serves as your guide to creating sustainable wealth and taking your finances to the next level. You will build a roadmap for your very own money success story. Buckle in, it's going to be a wildly profitable ride.

Disclosures:

This is the area for all of the Mama Lindsay tough love & legal stuff you need to know that my lawyer said I had to include so here we are, doing the thing.

There are going to be exercises for you to complete throughout this book. DO THEM. Not oh I'll go back and do them later. Orrr this isn't really that important can we just get to the strategy already. You are doing yourself a disservice. Every single page in this book was curated with intention. Every section builds on the one before it.

If you read this book with an open heart, an open mind, and really commit to doing the work, you WILL see a transformation. I also want to make a quick note to all the men reading this book. While this book was written with women in mind, it is a book for everyone. The english language uses "he" as the default pronoun, however it applies to women as well. So why can't we have a book for women that men read too? As Miki Agrawal would say, we can. While this book is not about feminism, in order to achieve true gender equality we need strong unity and partnership from our masculine allies. So let's all stand together as we heal ourselves and the world.

Before we begin, I'd like to challenge you. Challenge you to stand in loving disagreement with anything that doesn't sit well with you or brings up any level of resistance. Hold space for this, honor it, and when necessary, explore it further. Ask yourself why it is bringing up discomfort for you and if there is an underlying issue or element that needs healing. Take what you need from this at whichever level you are at. There is something in these pages for everyone at every stage of their journey. And you may want to revisit this later on when you find yourself at another stage in life. You are your best teacher.

I am not a financial advisor nor an attorney (yet). So you may want to consult your professional service providers before making any adjustments to your investment strategy or restructuring your portfolio. As a Corporate Accountant in my former life, I recognize many of these money moves will have tax implications. Finding the right strategy for you requires addressing numerous different factors, which we will discuss in more detail in the final section. After looking at your unique situation, they will advise you & help you create a plan 1:1 to maximize your investments. Don't have a financial advisor yet or not sure where to start? Don't worry girl, I got you. Keep reading & I'll give you some recommendations on navigating that in the section below

PART I

MONEY MINDSET & WHY IT IS ABOUT SO MUCH MORE

CHAPTER 1

MINDSET SHIFT

To shift your relationship with money, you must first become aware that your current relationship isn't serving you. Then you must do an inventory of your current belief system, values, and thus limiting beliefs. Lastly, you have to put in the WORK to dismantle and let go of beliefs that are no longer serving you and identify what really matters most to support the kind of life you want to lead. I'm not saying it's going to be easy. I'm just saying it's going to be worth it.

Reminder: We are going to dive deep and create a whole new set of beliefs around money. However, these new beliefs won't stick if you don't reinforce them with NEW habits and behaviors. Are you committed to implementing the shifts we identify together?

Say aye to declare you are ready to transform your relationship with money. Or if you're reading this on the train or hiding under your desk at work you can just turn the page…

CHAPTER 2

MINDFULNESS: TO BE AND NOT TO DO

Before we can go further, we have to get you out of the rat race. We are taught that if you aren't doing numerous things at once, you are wasting time. We are conditioned to be productive, and in turn relate our value as an individual to our ability to produce. Let me tell you right now, you were born to do more than work and die. Every single one of us was born with a God given right to be happy and whole. You don't have to earn it. You've already got all that you need. The challenge becomes unlearning all of society's false programming so you can tune into YOU. And one of the biggest lies fed to us from our environment that guides and shapes the way we interact with each other and the way we interact with money is the lie of scarcity...more on this shortly.

There is a screwed up western philosophy that you have to do and then get or have so you can eventually be. We really need to flip this on it's head. You must be first. You must be able to envision yourself living your highest potential raking in the dough. To see in your mind's eye that you have the power and the authority to step into your purpose and accomplish anything you will to be. We are co-creating with God. So you have to do your part in creating that vision if you expect to fully receive the fruit of the labor.

Who do you need to be to accomplish the things you long to accomplish? Get crystal clear on that and be super specific. Then start showing up as her NOW. Not tomorrow, not once you pay off all your debt and manifest $1M. You have to become this version of yourself in order to be able to make all of that possible.

CHAPTER 3

PERSONAL INVENTORY

What do you really want out of life? What are your values? Get REALLY honest with yourself. Don't be hard on yourself if this isn't easy to do at first. Again, we've been taught to keep our desires at bay to do what is expected of us. Remember those really ridiculous, confusing mixed signals we discussed earlier? Yeah, those expectations.

Start to do pleasure research exercises to figure out what brings you joy if you aren't sure already. What are those you may ask? Mama Gena in the book *School of Womanly*

Arts refers to them as a creative time where you give yourself the freedom to play and explore your desires and what lights you up. However, if you are ready to go and release your desires unto the world then by all means, please proceed. Below are a few exercises to help you get crystal clear on who you are, your values, and how you want to show up in the world:

1. Create a list of things that make you happy if you are not sure where to start - Insert Cheryl Crow lyrics **If it makes you happy, than it can't be that baaaaad.**

2. Ashley Stahl has a really great free-99 resource for establishing your core values. https://ashleystahl.com/wp-content/uploads/2016/11/Ashley-Internationals-CORE-VALUES.pdf

You can do this for your life and your business if applicable. I always recommend starting with your life FIRST, as everything that shows up in your business is a byproduct of YOU.

Establishing your values is the most important part. So don't move on to the next section until you've done this piece as we will be referring back to your values throughout the book. Once you've done the initial brain dump of your core values, do your best to limit it down to 10. Trust me, I know it's hard. But this will really help you to get crystal clear and ensure you are able to apply these values to your life and your relationship with money.

Here's a list of my values, brain dump and all, so you can get a feel for it and maybe a bit of inspiration:

My initial brain dump:
Respect
Equality
Hard Work
Honesty
Loyalty
Family & friends
Moral Code - high/strong moral fiber
Do gooder
My relationship with God
Collaboration

Creative & emotional expression
Reducing my carbon footprint
Finding sustainable solutions & alternatives
Human rights
Women's empowerment
Mentorship & Coaching
Diversity & rich cultural experiences
Mental Health Awareness

My Finalized 10 Core Values:
Connection
Responsibility
Spirituality
Family
Adventure
Radiance
Building
Mentorship
Honoring Myself
Integrity

If you are struggling with this, ask others what they would define as their values. You can even ask your close friends and family what they think your values are based on the way you are showing up in the world. Be sure to take any feedback you get with a grain of salt and remember that you have the final say. At the end of the day, no one can truly define your values and decide what you choose to do with them other than you.

Now let's align with em. Assess you behavior. Are you currently acting in alignment with these values? It's time to get REAL. Ask yourself what habits and relationships you are maintaining that are not aligned with the above value system.

STOP, drop em, & rollllll...okay I'll stop now. I just had to make sure you guys were still paying attention. This may mean you need to have some difficult conversations, clarify expectations, and create boundaries. Yes, even with your closest friends and family. Actually, I'd dare to say ESPECIALLY with your close friends and family. It's necessary and will save you so much time and energy in the long run. Which helloooo, means you have more time and energy to manifest all of the amazing things you desire, including money.

You have to make room for the awesomeness to come. Think of this like doing a little spring cleaning. Sure, it's uncomfortable at first. But once you get in the groove it's not so bad. And when it's all done, OH BOY does it feel good. You will be liberated and refreshed!

You must start acting and thinking like a wealthy person if you want to be one. And this isn't just about your finances. Everything is connected. It's all coming from YOU. So if you don't have your shit together & your mind right, you can't get your money right. Or your personal life, your career, or anything for that matter because YOU are at the cornerstone of all of that.

Now that you've clearly defined your values and started to make the necessary changes to align with them, let's dive into the most fundamental limiting belief when it comes to our relationship with money: the illusion of scarcity.

CHAPTER 4

THE LIE OF SCARCITY

We've all dealt with scarcity at some level or another in our lives. It doesn't matter if you're rich or poor, young or old, scarcity is an equal opportunity destroyer. It makes us feel like we are never enough. Will never have enough. Can never do enough.

To help us start to get a handle on this, I am proposing two models. One for the more tangible, physical aspects of life and money. This one is for the skeptics. I see you. I mean, I was you. So I get it. And the other for the more intangible, metaphysical aspects of life & money. For the believers who are ready to go all in and manifest abundance. I see you too. We are one.

The first model is transitioning from scarcity to sufficiency. There are three underlying myths in our society that perpetuate scarcity: **there is not enough for everyone, more is better**, and **that's just the way it is & there is nothing you can do about it**. We must begin to unravel these false truths if we ever hope to create sustainable wealth.

So we've all heard of going from scarcity to abundance mindset at one time or another. You may align with this, or if you're a bit more of a skeptic, maybe it sounds too good to be true. For those uncertain few, I suggest Lynne Twist's model of sufficiency. In her book *The Soul of Money,* she urges readers to become aware of the subconscious pull of scarcity within our society and provides a tangible alternative, sufficiency. That we are enough, we have enough, and when resources are allocated properly, we can thrive.

Scarcity mindset is used by the patriarchy (note, when I say patriarchy I am not referring to men. Men can be just as much victims of the patriarchy too - more on this later) as a form of control. To keep us down, scared, emotionally frazzled, and thus CONSUMING.

The second model takes us from scarcity to abundance. You may not know this, however, abundance is a mindset. Abundance is energy. It is not a physical state or destination as many may believe. Hear me out. If you are making 75K at a job and it isn't enough to you because it's not 100K, 200K, etc. That's on YOU. You are choosing to identify with the lack instead of the blessings. The scarcity or lack of abundance rather than the presence of abundance. You are giving abundance, or lack thereof, the meaning that is present in your life.

Now it's not totally your fault. You've been conditioned over the years by friends, family, the media, and other societal signals to view things from a lens of scarcity. Most of which are utilizing fear based tactics. And I don't know about you, but I refuse to make decisions and operate from a place of fear. Granted, it's not necessarily their fault either. The people who love you think they are helping you. They want to keep you "safe." I find this term to be quite relative, note the quotation marks.

From a cultural perspective, our society promotes the idea that success is having the biggest house, the nicest cars, and living this lavish lifestyle. The way people share only the highlight reel of their lives through social media just perpetuates these ideas and causes people to constantly compare themselves to others perceived "success". External validation is not the key to abundance. It's actually quite the opposite. Abundance cannot be found in the outside world, no matter how far and wide you look. True abundance starts from within.

To illustrate this further, think about relative ranges. Say you are making 75K as mentioned above. You get a raise to 80K. Now you can finally afford to make those improvements on your home or take on a slightly more expensive car payment. By the time you've made that one decision, you've already spent all the additional money from your raise. That is because as our income increases, our spending typically increases as well. So relatively speaking, you're not any richer or more abundant. You are actually just more reliant on that job you hate.

On the other hand, if you were making 75K and you got a 5K raise and decided to hold onto that money, to save it, create an emergency fund, or invest it, you would likely feel that you finally have a bit of breathing room. This in turn would create a mindset shift towards abundance.

In the sections that follow we will also discuss abundance from the intersection of spirituality and the laws of nature, so stay tuned for that.

CHAPTER 5

TOOLS FOR SHIFTING YOUR MINDSET

YOGA

Many people are intrigued by the benefits of meditation, however they claim they have tried and just can't get into it. They can't sit still, they can't calm their mind, whatever the case might be. I can totally relate. As a very high energy person who constantly functioned on overdrive, I swore I would never be able to sit still for more than a minute. And even that was a struggle. However, this all changed when I took a core and stretching class in college.

The teacher must have known her audience, because this was yoga in disguise. The first time I ever meditated was in this class. I was in shavasana, better known as corpse pose. I didn't even know I was meditating at first. We began each class with some movement to get the blood flowing and worked into some deep stretching and offset the stretches with core workouts. At the end of the class, we would wind down into corpse pose, turn off the lights, and lay there for 3-5 minutes. It was extremely relaxing, and most of the time I would be dozing off towards the end. Little did I know, I was meditating.

The idea that you have to be seated cross legged with gongs in the background and incense burning is quite the Hollywood adaptation. You can meditate anywhere in any position. Also, the western philosophy that you must be able to push everything out of your mind is too quite flawed. Meditation is less about forcing yourself to think of nothing and more about calming your mind and watching your thoughts pass by. Instead of being taken away and consumed by each thought, you start to become the observer. You watch the thoughts as they pass by, neither accepting or rejecting them, merely observing them. As if you were laying in the grass watching clouds float by in the sky.

Yoga, reading, running, weight training, all of these things can be an active form of meditation. As my husband says, when he is running he feels like he can out run his demons - IE his negative thought patterns and resistance. Determining what you need to achieve balance, for example a calm person might need something more stimulating, while a high energy person may need an activity more relaxing. This is key to finding your flow state.

As you become more acclimated with yoga or other forms of active meditation, you can begin to expand your practice. You can start to use it as a tool to guide your thoughts, set intentions, and manifest your wildest dreams. This level of self control is truly liberating. However, be patient with yourself as these things take time. As with most things in life, you should focus on the journey versus the outcome, taking your practice one day at a time.

MEDITATION

According to Merriam-Webster Dictionary, to meditate means 1 : to engage in contemplation or reflection IE He meditated long and hard before announcing his decision. 2 : to engage in mental exercise (such as concentration on one's breathing or repetition of a mantra) for the purpose of reaching a heightened level of spiritual awareness.[i]

For some of you this may mean prayer. You might use prayer as a form of meditation to contemplate & reflect on a scripture or sermon. It may mean praying as a form of connecting to God, your spiritual Father. You could also choose to repeat Biblical scriptures as your mantras.

For others it may mean creating quiet time and space to hear your thoughts. You may begin to notice the place between breaths and focus your attention on expanding those spaces as much as possible without strain. Some may choose to focus on a universal mantra such as om, while others might prefer to repeat a specific phrase or words of encouragement. One of my favorites is "rejection is divine redirection."

Regardless of how you choose to use meditation, have fun with it! Play around with different techniques and find the right fit for you. My rule of thumb when finding a practice that works for me is not too tight, not to loose. So try it on and see what works for you.

Before we dive into different forms of meditation, I would like to discuss the science behind meditation. You know I stay looking out for my skeptic friends...ehm, I mean analytical.

According to Rebecca Gladding, M.D. and clinical instructor and attending psychiatrist at UCLA, the brain without meditation operates predominantly from the Medial prefrontal cortex, often referred to as the "Me Center" and the Amygdala, or the "Fear Center." She states that "whenever you feel anxious, scared or have a sensation in your body (e.g., a tingling, pain, itching, whatever), you are far more likely to assume that there is a problem (related to you or your safety). This is precisely because the Me Center is processing the bulk of the information. What's more, this over-reliance on the Me Center explains how it is that we often get stuck in repeating loops of thought about our life, mistakes we made, how people feel about us, our bodies (e.g., "I've had this pain before, does this mean something serious is going on?) and so on."

In addition, the scientific observations from those who meditate regularly are quite intriguing. The connection between the Me Center and Fear Centers start to dissolve and a stronger, healthier connection begins to form between the Lateral prefrontal cortex, called the Assessment Center, which regulates your emotional response, and the Fear Center. This means that "your ability to ignore sensations of anxiety is enhanced as you begin to break that connection between the unhelpful parts of the Me Center and the bodily sensation/fear centers. As a result, you are more readily able to see those sensations for what they are and not respond as strongly to them."[ii] It also means you are able to look at situations and sensations from a place of rationality as well as increased empathy.

Emma Seppala, Ph.D, Science Director of the Center for Compassion and Altruism Research and Education at Stanford University & Faculty Director of the Yale School of Management's Women's Leadership Program, also says meditation "decreases pain, inflammation, depression, anxiety, and stress." She also states that meditation "improves memory, productivity, introspection, ability to regulate emotions and increases focus, attention, positive emotion, and social connection."[iii]

Sounds pretty freaking amazing, right?! Who wouldn't want that?

Okay, now that we've backed meditation with some serious SCIENCE, let's get back to it. For those of you who have been practicing mindful meditation for a while, a form of meditation focused on becoming present and increasing awareness, you may be ready to branch into other forms of meditation. Different kinds of meditation vary greatly depending on who you ask. Gaia.com, a member-supported media network of truth seekers and believers empowering an evolution of consciousness, describes the following forms of meditation:

Focused Meditation
Spiritual Meditation
Mantra Meditation
Transcendental Meditation
Movement Meditation
Mindful Meditation

Feel free to check out Gaia if you are seeking guided meditations to assist in your practice as they have a library of over 8,000 ad-free streaming videos.[iv]

Money is energy. It is a conduit for our highest commitments. If you want to know what somebody's values are and where their priorities lie, check their bank statement. So as we start to think of money as energy, as a frequency that we can tune into, things begin to change on a quantum level. You literally start to rewire your neural pathways and alter your DNA. Divine healing starts with you. For faith without works is dead, James 2:26. Meditation is how you start to tune your frequency. As you tune yourself into a frequency of prosperity, your energy begins to shift. Your thoughts begin to shift. You start to quiet your mind and create space for new, more positive ways of thinking and being to enter. Gradually, with consistent practice, your life begins to change. You can quite literally become a money magnet.

BREATHWORK

A good alternative if meditation and yoga aren't your thing. It's a great quick and active practice for those who say they can't quiet their mind or sit still. Also a wonderful compliment to any meditation or yoga practice to spice it up. Love me a good lion's breath, more on that to come...

So what the heck is breathwork? If you haven't tried this, it is going to change your life. It's so simple that anyone can do it. Yet it has so much utility and versatility that even yoga & meditation junkies can integrate this into their existing practice and see massive results.

Imagine trying to heal your emotions, calm your nerves and de-stress, with just logic alone. Pretty difficult, right? You overthink and run through all of these scenarios in your mind on repeat. What if instead you could just BREATHE.

Breathe and let your body do what it already knows how to do: take care of you & help you to heal.

The example I'm going to walk you through is an exercise I use all the time when I need a quick reset. Between coaching calls, during a long day of meetings, video recordings, etc. Imagine a cup of coffee without the anxiety and bad breath. Not hating on you coffee drinkers, drinking coffee on Saturday mornings or other times when I don't really need it is my guilt-free pleasure. And I LOVE a good dirty chai latte. Any who, back to the magic...

So we're going to do 3 sets of 10 and it only takes about 30 seconds. Start by taking a deep breath in. Then you are going to exhale out of your nose in brief little spurts while simultaneously flexing your abdomen. Do this for 10 counts. Once you've finished, we are going to do 10 short nasal breaths. Inhale through the nose and exhale through the nose, keeping your mouth closed. The inhale is a half count and the exhale is a half count, so again these are rather quick. And the final set is breath of fire or lion's breath. These will be a full count inhale and a full count exhale through the mouth. When you open your mouth to exhale, release an audible sound as you push out your breath.

Samantha Skelly, Founder of Pause Breathwork has a really cool Breathwork exercise you can check out for free online if you need a bit more guidance or want to try out an additional practice. There are many ways to breathwork! So feel free to play around with it. Sam also has a Certification Program called Hungry for Happiness for wellness coaches as well as Pause Breathwork facilitator training for those of you who want to integrate this practice into the healing work you do with yourself & others. The work she's doing in the world is seriously incredible!

JOURNALING

This is going to be a bit different than the usual journaling you may be thinking of, such as a thought catalog or a detailed record of your day. We're not talking about the diary you kept in 7th grade with all of your crushes and deepest secrets. I am talking about a whole different kind of journaling. Journaling to shift your money mindset and manifest wealth.

This exercise will help you start to identify negative thought patterns that are no longer serving you and places you might have blocks coming up. Once you've identified these limiting beliefs, then we are going to take it a step further and actually rewrite the narrative. I mastered this framework in Rachel Luna's Faith Activated Journaling Experience. Definitely check that out if you are looking for daily journal prompts, weekly devotionals, and a community of like-minded women of faith to support each other. The steps to this journaling practice are as follows:

Step 1: Brain Dump
Step 2: Mindset Shift
Step 3: Activate it

First, you brain dump all of your thoughts and feelings around a specific topic. Such as your relationship with money for example. And then you take a moment to analyze them. Where do you see limiting beliefs coming up?

Where are there opportunities for further introspection and healing? Think back to the values exercise we did at the beginning of this section. Do these notions align with your values?

Start to reframe these ideals in a way that supports you better. Where are the lies? And how can you reframe them to be in alignment with your truth. Your infinite potential. You may also want to find scriptures that reinforce the truth through God's word if that is aligned with your beliefs. For example, if the feeling that you are not enough or not worthy of holding wealth keeps coming up for you, you can find scriptures where God is declaring your rightful place in prosperity and abundance, such as Jeremiah 33:6 ESV "Behold, I will bring to it health & healing and I will heal them & reveal to them abundance of prosperity & security."

Once you have identified these blocks, now comes the fun part. You then rewrite the entire journal entry. Be sure to use present or past tense verbs such as "it feels so good" or "it felt so good when" as if it's already happened. This time, use the new language you came up with during the reframing portion. You quite literally shift the ideas that you hold around this topic and solidify it in writing. This helps your brain start to create new pathways for fresh new ways of thinking and release old, harmful thoughts that are no longer serving you.

I won't bore you with all of the neuroscience and technical lingo, unless you're into that. Then check out this article from Forbes.[v] Otherwise, just trust me. This seriously works. And it's time you use the tools to manifest financial prosperity and heal your money trauma. You are not helpless over your money situation, you just have to ACTIVATE the mindset shift around money. And faith activated journaling is the first step.

Don't just take my word for it though. Try it for yourself! That way the breakthroughs and results will be abundantly clear. Here are a few journal prompts to try on your own and get you started:

How do I begin to view money as an energy exchange?
How is money connected to my self worth?

Where do the money blockages live in my body? What have I been avoiding in my finances?

Give those a try and let me know what is coming up for you. Feel free to share in our Boss Women Facebook group https://www.facebook.com/groups/henryettas/. I can't wait to hear about the transformations you are able to accomplish through this incredible practice! The results will show sometimes immediately. I'm talking the same day or the day after. And I say this from personal experience. I've manifested clients, support, partnerships, and miraculous healing from committing to this practice. Especially once you get into a good flow and are journaling consistently. The manifestations will be abundant! We'll talk more about manifesting too in the section that follows.

However, don't beat yourself up if you aren't seeing results right away. Sometimes these beliefs are so ingrained into our subconscious minds that it takes a few tries to fully uproot them and start to rewire our thought patterns. And that's okay too. Healing is a journey, so be gentle with yourself. Show yourself some compassion and be grateful to be on this beautiful ride. Grateful to have the ability to do this work and to heal. For yourself, for all of humanity, and for future generations. Because we all rise as a collective in consciousness when we heal on an individual level.

Before we wrap up this section, I have to mention another specific kind of journaling that is a crucial element to any healing practice. And that is Gratitude Journaling. Gratitude journaling is the practice of making a list of things you are grateful for. Many suggest doing this at the end of the day as a form of reflection. I recommend a minimum of three things you are grateful for. Once you get in a good flow with this you will likely have much more than three items on your list.

According to a study by researchers from the University of Minnesota and the University of Florida, "having participants write down a list of positive events at the close of a day -- and why the events made them happy -- lowered their self-reported stress levels and gave them a greater sense of calm at night." I personally prefer to do gratitude journaling and prayer first thing in the morning. Before I get out of bed, before I check my phone, before I do anything, I make a note of at least three things I'm grateful for, though often the list is much longer. This helps me create positive thoughts & energy first thing in the morning to prime my day ahead.

This is something I utilized long before I was fully immersed in my healing journey. Gratitude journaling was recommended to me in undergrad by one of my professors and mentors when I sustained a pretty bad injury. I had a bucket handle meniscus tear, was out of school for two weeks and work for two months, and spiraled into a pretty bad depression. It really helped and was one of the first journaling exercises I stuck with as an adult.

MANIFESTING

To manifest quite literally means to be evidence of or to prove. So in this way, a manifestation doesn't mean you thought of something, you want it, and now you are going to create it. It's more than that. It means it already is. And all you are doing is providing evidence to show yourself and others it's truth. In other words, you're just verifying what you already know to be true. So in order to effectively manifest, you cannot be coming from a place of lack or feeling without. "Oh I need this" or "I want that" is not the pathway to successful manifesting. Manifesting is about tuning into what already is. We will cover this in a bit more detail when we talk about the Law of Attraction in sections below. For now, just keep in mind that everything you want is already yours.

One way to tune into this is through visualization. Visualization is an element of manifesting that incorporates a style of mediation. It allows you to get familiar with what accomplishing that goal or dream will look like and how it will feel. To understand this, you put yourself in a state of mind where the goal has already been reached. You see yourself crossing the finish line and celebrating with all of your friends and family, either literally or metaphorically.

If you'd like to take it a step further, ask yourself what you will be able to do or accomplish now that the goal has been met. For example, now that I have run my first marathon, I know I am unstoppable. I know that I have so much more strength and resilience than I ever thought was possible.

My confidence is at an all time high and I am ready to start crossing other items off of my bucket list. This experience has empowered me to eat healthy, look good, feel good. To stay disciplined and consistent in ways I didn't even know were possible. I feel the best I have ever felt in my life. I feel like I could do anything!

Now start to tune into this frequency. And realize that it is not some far away thing. It is not some lofty goal that you cannot accomplish. It is here, right now. Ready to be brought into your vibrational frequency. Ready to share it's love and light with you. It's already yours. All you have to do is tune into it and then take action that aligns you with it. If you can see it in your minds eye, then you can hold it in your hand.

There is abundance beyond your wildest imagination queued up and ready to be released to you. What you have to do is practice the vibration of it, and it will make its way to you. That's what trips most people up. For the most part, we don't practice the vibration of our desires. We practice the vibrations of our environment and what has already been manifested.

You've got to quit focusing so much on what already is to the point that it controls your vibrational patterns and frequency output. Instead focus on who you really are and how you want to feel. Abundance attracts abundance.

Another key element is to tune into your feelings. These feelings are an emotional compass or dial to your intuition. To your highest self and your soul. What does it feel like when I am that *insert your desires here *. When that's who I am. When that's what I'm living.

What does it feel like when you envision the following:

What does security feel like?
What does having an impact feel like?
What does worthiness feel like?
What does accomplishing your wildest dreams feel like?
What does leaving a legacy feel like?

Think about why else you care about money. What does having money bring you? Then start to tune into the vibrational frequency, the emotion that attaining that prosperity brings you. Then you can start to bring what is already yours into your life. To see it in the physical and align with it in the present moment.

Affirmations are another way to reinforce the manifestation process. Always speak or write from the present tense. IE I AM confident, I AM a New York Times Bestselling author, I AM using my finances to align with my soul's purpose and highest commitments. Speak on it like it's already happened or is happening. This is key to effectively affirming what your soul already knows to be true.

Listen to my complimentary **Guided Meditation: Manifest Wealth & Prosperity** here: http://www.wealthmeditation.healmoneytrauma.com/home32175802

PART II

EMOTIONAL & SPIRITUAL HEALING

CHAPTER 6

RELATIONSHIPS WITH OTHERS & THE SELF

The first thing I want to say is you are worthy of miraculous healing. Your trauma is worthy, your story is worthy, your pain is worthy. And I am here for you. We are all here for you. Me and every single woman reading this book and healing their money trauma alongside you. It is through this fierce sisterhood, a safe space for you to open up and start to unpack the trauma, that you will truly heal.

We see you, we honor you, we acknowledge you.

And we want you to know you are not alone.

My heart goes out to you for the pain you have been through. The isolation and loneliness it must have caused as you suffered alone. But you're not alone anymore. And we are going to do this together.

CHAPTER 7

TRAUMA

Trauma is any experience that causes physical, emotional, spiritual, or psychological harm. Examples of commonly recognized trauma may include the loss of a loved one, a divorce, a car accident, etc. However, trauma encompasses much more than these extreme cases. It can also include experiences such as watching your parents fight about money as a kid. Losing your job or juggling excessive amounts of debt as you struggle to make ends meet just to pay your bills. Money and finances are often the most fearful, stress-ridden element of our lives.

Moreover, financial stressors are often a trauma we feel we can't escape from. When we are faced with extreme amounts of stress, our body enacts a fight or flight mode. This response was created to protect us from environmental dangers such as an attack from a wild animal. Once the situation was over, our bodies would return to a normal homeostasis. However, with money trauma there is no downtime. It locks our adrenal glands into overdrive. So essentially, you are constantly on high alert. Operating in this way is not sustainable. Your body wasn't built for it. This in turn leads to burnout, depression, anxiety, and use of unhealthy coping mechanisms such as drug & alcohol abuse. The list goes on and on.

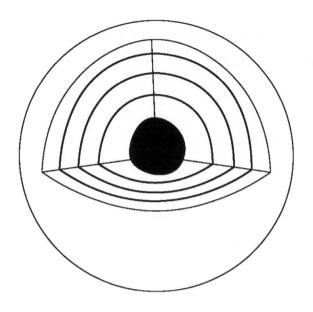

The trauma, or wound, has layers of adverse emotions on top of it to protect you from the deepest pain associated with the traumatic experience, as pictured above. Your ego uses these layers of emotions to cover or create a barrier to "protect" the trauma from causing us any further pain. This is often why people who go through horrendous experiences such as sexual trauma at a young age don't even remember it until much later in life. Their minds have actually buried the trauma so deep it is not easily accessible.

These protection layers of emotion include disgust, shame, sadness, overwhelm, fear, anger, hate, and ultimately self hate to name a few. These may show up for you slightly differently. They may also be rearranged as you start to uncover the layers of protection on your healing journey.

The pain from this trauma is showing up both inside of you and outside of you. On the outside, it may manifest as trust issues. It could also manifest as judgement towards others. The projections are endless. Even though you can see the pain outside of you, you must go deep within yourself in order to truly heal.

As you start to look within yourself in the following pages, begin to direct your awareness to where you are in the healing cycle. Start to acknowledge where you find yourself looping or getting stuck in the trauma cycle. For once we start to bring these patterns into our conscious mind, they no longer have power over us.

There is one other thing I would like to address before we move forward. As we talk about healing within the context of this book, it is important to note that we are talking about healing with the intention of achieving alignment. Otherwise, you may find yourself stuck in a feedback loop of identifying trauma and become addicted to finding something to work on or fix. If you love a good project, redo your kitchen. Help your neighbor with their yard. You don't need to become a spiritual hypochondriac and constantly be on the mend just to be a healer. There is a whole world out there, so don't get lost in the rabbit holes of your own mind forever. It's about healing trauma to become whole, not just for the sake of healing itself.

CHAPTER 8

THE EGO & ASKING FOR HELP

The ego is a seat housed within the self. It's a place of "I" and serves a very important role in self preservation & survival. The ego often gets a bad wrap. However, it's actually the protector. Kind of like your big brother. Even though he can be a total jerk, you know he just wants to protect you. Your ego also represents material existence and is there to take care of business.

There are a few basic principles that the Ego operates from. These include fear of death, time and space are the only reality, we are all separate and operate independently, and if it's not material than it doesn't exist. So in essence, your ego either leaves no room for God or thinks it is God. Have you ever heard of the acronym for EGO - Edging God Out?

The Self on the other hand knows death is an illusion. Time and space are mere constructs and we are all connected. Ultimately, love is all that matters and God is all there is. Infinite planes of reality exist - created by, sustained by, and infused by the spirit of God. As such, the two are at a constant war with each other. This may leave you feeling conflicted, confused, and if left unattended can cause extreme cognitive dissonance.

In his book, *theWARofART*, Steven Pressfield defines the strongest enemy of, and within, our consciousness as resistance. Resistance is the Ego's greatest weapon against the Self. Why is this? Because the less we change and evolve, the more we rely on the Ego. So the Ego summons the troops in the form of resistance to sabotage your evolution. Which means the Ego is preserved and everything stays the same. On the other hand, the more awakened we become, the less we need the Ego. As we reconnect with the Self we touch upon Divine Ground, finding true meaning in our existence and co-creating our evolutionary future.[vi]

Now that we have an understanding of the Ego and the strategy it uses to maintain its power, let's discuss one of the greatest assets of advocating for the Self: asking for help.

Asking for help is a toughie. It's tough because there are times where our ego prevents us from asking for the help we actually need. Then there are also times where our ego feeds resistance with fear and insecurity, making us feel like we need help from others when we don't. So how the hell do you decipher the two? One simple word: meditation. In order to decipher what messages are your own, you must quiet the space in your mind. You can't even hear the whisper of your intuition, the native language of the Self, if 20 different voices are talking over it. These voices may be your own ego, your friends, your parents, colleagues, your significant other...the list could be endless. So the prerequisite to asking for help is to quiet your mind and ask yourself if you really need the help or if you already have the answer you seek.

If you have an answer and you are just second guessing yourself or "overthinking" and allowing other people's opinions of you to get in the way, then stop that. Make a resolve in that moment to let go of the external validation and trust yourself. After all, you know you and what you want better than anyone else. On the other hand, if you do this exercise and realize you do in fact still need help, then go get it. Ask a trusted advisor, mentor, a friend, or a family member whose opinion you value. Be mindful of the topic or expertise needed and be sure you are seeking help from people qualified to help you.

On the other hand, if you are just looking for a forum to complain or delay actually taking any action, stop right there and get right with yourself first. Don't waste your time, or anyone else's. If you just need to express yourself emotionally, let off steam, or be heard there is nothing wrong with that. Just be mindful that you aren't overindulging or placing too much negativity onto any one person. For example, if you know that every time you are annoyed with Sharon at work you call your friend Brandy, then stop that. Think about how you would feel if you were in Brandy's shoes. Your friend only calls you when they want to complain, always asks for advice, and never takes it. That would get a little exhausting, right?

We are all living our own unique human experiences, interwoven into each others stories sharing similar emotions and thoughts. So remember to be respectful to others in the same way you want respect shown to you when asking for help. We are all in this together, and no one should suffer alone. Surround yourself with people who are "we" people, as eager to help you as you are to help them. That way when you need a little support, you have options and are not forced to constantly go to the same person. And remember if you need additional support from a community of women all over the world, check out the FB Group www.facebook.com/groups/henryettas.

CHAPTER 9

THE EMOTIONAL PAIN BODY

According to Eckhart Tolle in *The Power of Now*, "every emotional pain that you experience leaves behind a residue of pain that lives on in you. It merges with the pain from the past, which was already there, and becomes lodged in your mind and body. This, of course, includes the pain you suffered as a child, caused by the unconsciousness of the world into which you were born."[vii]

Tolle believes that the only way to dissolve the emotional pain body is through presence. Bringing your full awareness to what you are experiencing or feeling sheds a conscious light onto the shadows of your ego. This is because its survival depends on your unconscious identification with it, as well as on your unconscious fear of facing the pain that lives in you. The more that you avoid it, the more it grows.

So how does this show up for you? One way is through triggers, or things that may be inconsequential to someone else, yet really seem to bother you. In order to understand this, we must acknowledge that thoughts and feelings can be misleading. They have the power to take us captive if we do not make an intentional choice to engage in conscious behavior. We often draw up elaborate schemes and narratives. Defending ourselves, judging others, whatever it takes to avoid taking responsibility and place the blame on others instead. We are often reliving a past experience through engaging in these old thought patterns. The past is familiar, so we would rather stay in the past than branch into the unknown of the future. That's further evidence to why tuning into the present moment is so important. Living in the past causes pain. Living in the future causes anxiety. The only true place to be at peace, to be whole, is the present.

Reacting, similar to being triggered, is when you feel an emotional response to something someone has said or done and you instantly snap back without even thinking about it. Almost like a knee jerk reaction. It's often a recreation of an old pattern of behavior or a previous timeline. Something the "old you" would do if you will. Responding on the other hand is thoughtful and intentional. You take your time to process what the other person has said or done before you make a conscious choice of how you would like to respond. This method of communication usually results in defusing the situation and honoring yourself and the other party.

In order to shift from reacting to responding, you have to pause. Sometimes this means you pause for a moment, other times it may mean you wait a few days before responding. Believe it or not, you don't have to answer that text from your ex right away. They can wait. And you will thank yourself that you held off until you're able to formulate an intentional response. Otherwise, you are often giving away your power. You are allowing the other person to get the best of you. And more times than not, that's exactly what they want. Control. To keep you stuck in old patterns, ways of thinking, and behaviors so they can hold on to the idea of what once was. My best recommendation for how to overcome this power struggle is to breath. Breath, and remember who the f*ck you are, you beautiful goddess.

CHAPTER 10

BEING AN EMPATH

Do you feel extremely sensitive to external stimuli? When a friend comes to you with a problem, can you feel their pain? And I don't mean you can imagine it, I mean you can feel the stabbing sensations in the pit of your stomach as if you were the one being faced with this dilemma. If this sounds like you, chances are you're an empath. And even if you aren't, you are very likely to encounter close relationships with those who are, such as your significant other, children, close friends, etc.

Feeling everyone else's emotions so deeply can be a very difficult burden to bare. However, when handled responsibly, being an empath is one of the greatest gifts you could ever take part in. It allows you to truly understand others, to support them in their needs, and to help them overcome obstacles and difficult circumstances. Getting to this point of self mastery can certainly be a challenge though. Feeling overwhelmed in large groups of people, getting physically ill from the stress experienced by others, soaking up everyone else's energy like a sponge, it can be exhausting. Trust me, I know. I did it for years.

That's why you have to zip it up. I mean this metaphorically, although I have absolutely exercised it in quite the literal way as well, especially at first. What I mean by this is that you have to "zip it up" and create an invisible barrier between yourself and others emotions. Think of it like a screen door. You aren't closing off the outside world completely. You still want to see outside and allow others to enter when you grant them permission. However, you don't want every pesky mosquito and moth to swarm into your home. So the screen door keeps them out.

In the more literal sense, I recommend envisioning an invisible bee suit of sorts that you have to "zip up" before you start your day, before you go visit family for the holidays, or deal with any other person's emotionally riveting circumstances. This allows you to be there to support your friends and family, without allowing yourself to be consumed and dragged down by the weight of their emotional baggage. Once you have gotten this down, you can start to master your empathic abilities and control the power like a volume knob to turn it up or turn it down as needed through the lens of compassion.

CHAPTER 11

LAW OF ATTRACTION

While we are on the topic of being conscious of the energy we take in, let's discuss being aware of the energy we are putting out. You may be asking yourself what energy has to do with money...well, everything. Money is energy. It is something we made up long ago and we all decided it has "x" value and so it does. It used to be backed by the gold standard, meaning the value was matched by something. However, we did away with that nearly 100 years ago and now we've replaced it with fiat money. Fiat is latin for "let it be done." So essentially, money is nothing more than energy and it only holds the amount of energy, or value, we assign to it.

We all emit energy through a vibrational frequency. Just like sound waves or light waves. Like magnets or numerous other scientific laws of the universe. If you tune in to the frequencies of your dreams, the frequency of abundance, you will come into alignment with them and bring them to you much faster. Another way to think of this is a path of least resistance.

Now ask yourself what that feels like. For me, it feels like clarity. It feels unlimited. It feels infinite. It feels fun. Now I understand it isn't always easy to feel like money is unlimited. Start somewhere else if you need to. Take money out of the equation. Where else do you feel abundance? Where else do you feel joy?

If you can get into the general idea, the feeling of why you want this, it becomes much easier. Why do you want money? Is it to provide more opportunities for your children? Now imagine what it feels like to provide those opportunities. Is it to travel the world and serve others?

Imagine how that feels. Tune into the vibrational frequency of why you want this money, and how good that feels to know this is what is coming to be. Tune into the joy, into the soul behind why you want money in the first place.

You can practice the vibration of the manifestation that is on its way to you at anytime. Everything you've asked for is coming. The only question is how long are you going to keep yourself from it? How long are you going to put out the frequency of lack? The frequency of feeling without? You cannot expect to bring anything else to you outside of what you believe to be possible. If all you see is problems, all you are going to be able to receive is problems. It's the only thing you have your radio dialed into. You can't hear the wealth frequency on 98.7 when you are listening to the scarcity frequency on 105.9. Do you get what I'm saying?

As mentioned, sometimes you have to leave money out of the equation at first. Sounds crazy, right? However, the energy that you are putting out, the energy of stress, of worrying, of going without is perpetuating your circumstance. You are putting out an energy of lack. An energetic void if you will. The signal or frequency you are putting out to the universe is saying I am without. So this is all you will ever receive.

Is this starting to make sense? Whether intentional or not, you are asking the universe to withhold wealth from you. And sure, you might say well how can I have a vibration of wealth and prosperity if I've never know what that feels like. Well, think again. Have you ever felt good? Those moments where it could all end right then and that would be alright because you would go happy? That is wealth. That is prosperity. That is what it's like to be whole. And at the end of the day money can't do that for you. YOU have to do that for you.

Money is nothing more than a conduit for your highest commitments. So if you aren't committed to your wellbeing, to becoming whole, than money isn't going to do that for you either. It will just come and go. Or be another means to an end.

Your happiness, your wholeness, that has to be the goal. Not financial wealth for the sake of being rich. Not making a bunch of money so other people will like you or validate your existence. Your alignment with your highest self has to be the intention. Once this is your true goal, the high frequency of alignment will cause the conditions around you to change. As soon as you put feeling good as your top priority, everything else will fall into place. This is your power.

Joy spreads. Positivity spreads. Light spreads. Love is the purest vibration that there is, and this radiates to others. Think about it this way. In the atmosphere of worship, the presence of God is palpable. The Glory, The Greatness, The Majesty, The Wonders, and The Goodness come alive in moments of worship. This is feeling the vibration of God. And this feeling amplifies God's energy. It exudes God's love.

So in order to align with God's will for your life, in order to align with abundance, you must tune into how it feels. How does it feel to make tons of money? How does it feel to manifest your wildest dreams and live your best life? How does it feel to heal your money trauma and integrate prosperity into your life? How does it feel to create sustainable wealth for you and your family? Really start to visualize achieving all of this and tuning into how it feels to live a wildly profitable life.

Do you know how much money is in your vortex? A vortex being a vibrational holding place for all of the rockets of desire you've ever launched. The Bigger Plan that God has for you that you can hardly even comprehend. It is INSANE. Especially when you have experienced so much pain around the areas of your finances. That contrast of what you know to be true to who you are in your soul, who God has called you to be, is so stark relative to what you are experiencing that it's causing a storm. So let's bring on the rain! Because we all know what happens after the storm.

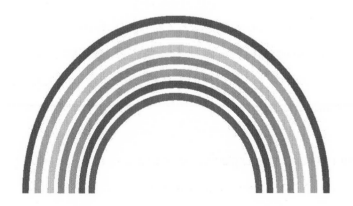

CHAPTER 12

CHILDHOOD TRAUMA

Before we dive in, I want you to acknowledge that you will likely have to exercise some serious compassion and forgiveness as we dive into your childhood trauma. My personal healing journey required a lot of forgiveness. So we'll dive into forgiveness in intimate detail shortly after. I'll tell you more about my biggest childhood trauma in that section also.

We all go through experiences during our upbringing that are traumatic. Some of us much more than others.

However, the human mind, and particularly the child's mind, sees trauma a bit differently. We as adults would often only consider the most extreme circumstances such as physical or sexual abuse for example, a trauma. Yet as a child you were much more susceptible to experiencing deep wounds. Something as seemingly insignificant as your parents going on a week vacation and leaving you with your grandparents could cause trauma. Your child self may have thought, why don't they want to be with me? Is there something wrong with me? Why have they left me all alone? Do they not love me anymore? While we as adults have the sensibility to rationalize these thoughts, the child's mind is still forming. It is experiencing emotions, many of which for the first time, and it hasn't quite learned the ability of discernment and critical thinking.

These thoughts and feelings hurt us. They take root in our emotional core, our Inner Child. If left untreated, they can sabotage our relationships with ourselves and others. This is something that many refer to as the Outer Child. In other words, this is when our Inner Child lashes out and becomes apparent in our behavior as an adult. Perhaps your significant other has asked for a bit of space. This could be for a perfectly logical reason, such as they have a big project coming up at work and they really need to focus. However, your Inner Child might be triggered by this experience if you have unresolved emotions regarding an experience in your childhood which you perceived as abandonment, such as the example of parents taking a vacation above. So instead of handling the situation logically and practically, you lash out. You get offended, take it personally, cry and scream at them that you might as well just end it because clearly this isn't working, in a hope that you may leave them before they can leave you.

This "protector" defense mechanism occurs when we have an unresolved emotional experience, or trauma, which our Ego deems was so painful that we must do whatever it takes not to experience that again. So these protector emotions cause us to act out of alignment with what we really want or what we really need to overcome or heal this trauma at its core.

In this circumstance, what the individual really wants is to be loved. To be embraced and supported and to know that you are never going to leave. That they will never be abandoned or alone. However, what they are communicating externally is that they don't need anyone else, that they are independent and don't take any shit. They are pushing others away before others can do it to them, purely out of self defense. Knowing this, both about ourselves and about others, empowers us to do something about it.

This can apply to our relationships with money as well. If you were traumatized by poverty growing up, such as myself, this could be affecting the way you interact with money today. This might show up as scarcity. You may feel like you can't take risks because you have to prioritize your security. For me, it's manifested in the form of feeling unworthy of holding wealth. I was so used to making a dollar stretch, being frugal, and living without that I didn't know how to be wealthy. Or understand how it felt to be wealthy. I could hardly even accept being comfortable for that matter. It felt surreal to me. I was just waiting for something terrible to happen to put me back into the trauma cycle and back into poverty.

After a lot of deep work, journaling, prayer, meditation, and reframing I have been able to overcome these limiting beliefs. I know I am worthy of holding wealth. Not only am I worthy of holding wealth, it is my divine birthright. It is an honor and a privilege to share this wealth of knowledge I've learned along on my own path. Both as an accountant and just as a human with the same feelings, traumas, & ups and downs we all face. I'm not perfect, nor do I claim to be. I am still on my own journey and I am learning every day. However, I can certainly share with you what has helped me to heal my money trauma so that we can create sustainable wealth together.

Before we dive deeper, I feel called to mention something that is essential to understand. These experiences are not a burden. They quite literally made you who you are. And that's beautiful. These experiences and traumas are an opportunity. An opportunity to learn. An opportunity to grow. An opportunity to heal.

From another perspective, perhaps your parents often fought over money and were unsure of how they were going to pay the bills. This too could affect the way you feel about money. The energy of conflict, or fear of it, could be forcing its way into your relationships and spending habits. You avoid managing your finances altogether because it subconsciously becomes an element of pain or suffering. You begin to normalize the idea that people fight over money and this becomes a theme in your relationship with your significant other.

No one wants to live this way. A victim to our circumstances, replaying the same episode of our parents poor spending habits or failed marriage. By no means am I saying you should blame your parents. I'm saying that you should identify these themes when they are present and understand that you have a choice. A choice of whether to fall victim to those same patterns and behaviors that lead to scarcity and conflict or to choose differently. We have more than enough resources in this day and age to accomplish anything we set out to. We have the wisdom and tools to truly heal. All it takes is a choice. There is enough. You are enough. You deserve to be empowered by your finances, not debilitated by them.

If you recognize these behavioral patterns within yourself, I highly recommend taking the time to do some Inner Child healing work. I'll include some additional reference points for this in the resources section. If you recognize these behavioral patterns in others, well...that's a bit more complicated. Granted, this will depend on the individual, but people are often defensive and feel attacked regarding deeply rooted emotional issues. They tend to feel like it's not their fault and that you must be blaming them some how to even bring it up. So proceed with caution. I recommend starting slowly and see how receptive they are to it. For example, perhaps the next time you feel like their Outer Child is lashing out, ask them how they feel. Ask them if there is anything they would like to talk about. Or even better, share with them a story of a time when you were reacting a certain way but really meant or felt something else, such as your own emotional trauma or Inner Child work. Share your own story and guide them through your own personal experience before attempting to address the issue head on. You must first create an element of trust, a sort of safe container for them to feel like it's okay to open up and share. Gauge how receptive they are to it.

This deep work is not something you can force on anyone. It is hard, emotionally grueling, painful stuff and not everyone is ready for that level of responsibility. And that's okay. However, if they are receptive to it, then take baby steps. Provide them with an article to read or connect them with someone you know who has trainings and discussions around the topic. Ask them if they would like support in this area. If they are receptive, then perhaps you two can support each other through the healing process. It can be very emotionally exhausting, so having a proper support system is crucial. Join us in the FB Group if you need to find an accountability partner:

https://www.facebook.com/groups/henryettas/

Also, quick disclosure. Don't go pointing out anyone else's trauma, or even trying to help them heal their own Childhood Trauma, until you've begun your own healing journey. Otherwise, you are just using someone else's pain as a distraction from your own. Which typically results in projection, frustration, resentment, and so on. Healing is like the in-flight safety spiel. You know what I'm talking about. You must put the oxygen mask on yourself first before you can help others to heal.

So once you've done your own work and you are spreading that love and light to others, what do you do if they aren't receptive? Well, you love them anyway. We all have free will, and we are all on our own unique paths. Maybe they are not ready for that phase of their journey yet, and that's okay. Just calmly let them know that if and when they would like to explore their Inner Child and Childhood Trauma that you are there to support them in any way you can. This doesn't mean you should tolerate dysfunctional behavior if they are lashing out at you and others. Healthy boundaries are a necessary element for any relationship to thrive. It just means you have to let them heal at their own pace and not try to control their pace or trajectory.

CHAPTER 13

ANCESTRAL KARMA & GENERATIONAL BELIEFS

Traditions and beliefs around money get passed down in the same way oppression, false truth and hierarchy do. It perpetuates the system and keeps the mass consciousness a lower, dense level. This is the permeating effects of the patriarchy attempting to maintain control. Disclosure: when I say the patriarchy, I am not referring to men. Men too are victims of the patriarchy. These are your brothers, your partners, your fathers, your sons. They aren't bad people, and they love you. The patriarchy is specifically the imbalance of masculine energy in relation to the overall picture. We need masculine energy, however we need feminine energy as well in equal parts. In government, in leadership, in corporate America, you name it. And what we are seeing right now in the world, the hate, murder, injustice, and PAIN, is because of this concentration of power within the patriarchal system. Did you know that only 6% of the world's leaders are female? If you want to know how to save the planet and nurture humanity back to balance, try putting more women in positions of power.

I know I went on a bit of a tangent, but it was necessary to give context and remind you why it's not your parents, or even their parents fault that they had messed up relationships around money. They didn't know any better. But you do. And that's why you're here. Reading this book and putting in the work. Because you are going to break the cycle.

I'd like to share a story with you about how this has shown up for me. Allow me to set the stage. Internalizing these feelings, such as the ones described above, and watching them present themselves to me at 10:30 am on a Saturday morning at a Healing the Wound Meditation & Astrology class by Malorine Mathurin and Markus Winter.

As we eased into the meditation, Michael asked us to visualize our trauma or pain as an animal. And often what comes up during this experience is actually layers, or protector emotions, covering up the trauma so that it can't hurt you again. This is one of your body and mind's many self defense or coping mechanisms.

I began to see a large black cat surrounded by total darkness. It's snarls began before I could even see it's face. The large feline ferociously reared its fangs and cried out once more in rage. I recognized that this was my anger.

Just as soon as that awareness came into my consciousness, the images began to shift. I saw an elk walking into a forest and decided to follow it. As we made our way into a clearing, the elk started to shrink. Its horns got smaller and smaller until they were no longer, and the animal began to transfigure into a small doe.

I walked closer to the deer and stretched out my hand. She was skittish at first. She backed away a few times before walking towards me ever so slowly with her head lowered. As she got closer, I realized the animal had a wound.

She whimpered as I drew nearer to the wound. It looked like a bullet hole above the top left shoulder. Almost instinctively, I began to dislodge the bullet. She cried out but stayed firm, glad to have someone to help her heal this unhealable wound.

Almost as soon as the obstruction was removed, the wound began to heal. A glowing light brought the fur back together again, and within a few minutes the doe began to stand.

As I reached down to pet it, it began to shrink. So I picked it up and held it close to my chest as we shared our unconditional love in this moment together. Tears began to pour down my face as I took in everything I had just experienced. I immediately understood what each of these messages meant when they were shown to me. The first animal, the Bobcat or Jaguar, represented my anger.

I felt angry. Angry at the world that my anger wasn't socially acceptable enough to be expressed. Angry at my family for shying away from or shaming my anger. Angry at myself for feeling this anger as well as angry for allowing all of these factors to get to me and cause me to hide or suppress my anger. Most importantly, I felt angry for having the very problem I was protecting in the first place: my pain. There was a part of me who saw the expression of this pain as some sort of weakness. When I expanded on this further, I uncovered a slew of trauma around my conditioning, the patriarchal role, family karma, and childhood trauma.

To give you a glimpse into my childhood, we lived in poverty growing up. My mother was a single mom. While she worked extremely hard at multiple jobs to provide for my brother Taylor and I, she could barely make ends meet. She made countless sacrifices so that we could have the things we wanted. She always put herself on the back burner and focused instead on what and who we needed her to be. Let me tell you though, she sure as hell knew how to stretch a dollar.

When I got older, I felt like I had no one to talk to about money. I was eager to learn all of the best strategies, build my credit, and put myself on a trajectory of financial success. I went to the bank when I was 17 to open my first account and learn how to be financially savvy. The only person in my life that seemed to have a handle on their finances was my grandmother, so I had her cosign for me to open my first account.

However, the more I discussed finances with my grandmother, the more I realized a key breakdown. She was wealthy because she pinched pennies and put away as much money as she could, but she didn't have her money working for her. She was holding herself back from true wealth because she was unwilling to trust. She was afraid to give anything away. And you have to be able to give if you wish to receive.

This hoarding of precious resources went far beyond finances. My grandmother had withheld the very love and care that my mother needed to become the strong woman she was meant to be. I'm pretty sure my mom was 30 before she heard the words "I love you" from her own mother. So instead of setting my mom up for success, she set my mom up for years of pain and trauma spent seeking the very love that was withheld from her. After years of heartache, my mother poured this unconditional love into my brother and I.

As my mom's mother became a grandmother and witnessed the beauty of this unconditional love unfold, she began to open her heart and realize what she had been missing. What she had greedily withheld from my mother, she then wanted to give to us. Although to be honest, she wasn't very good at it. She never seemed to me to be the kind of grandmother you bake cookies with and get warm hugs from that gets depicted in sitcoms or that "other families" had. She was cultured and liked to discuss grandiose ideas, accomplishments, or the global news. However, I will say she showed affection in her own way.

This pattern of behavior however, the removal of the unconditional love my mother needed to develop into a strong, autonomous, fully connected adult caused a sort of ostracization. In my mother's childhood, my grandmother grew resentful of her for getting in the way. Which is only to be expected when you are withholding love and thus not fully connected to your family and others. This caused my mother to quite literally be the victim and induced trauma in her most developmental years around connection and receiving the love she needed. It also forced her into autonomy far before she was ready or able.

The more I unpacked this, the more I felt for my mother. The more my own resentment towards her came to light and began to heal. I realized I was blaming her for being the victim when it wasn't her fault. Granted, I am not saying it was necessarily my grandmothers either. She had more than her own fair share of childhood trauma including Polio at the age of 11. The time during puberty when women's bodies are developing into what they will be into adulthood and self-worth is being formed as a byproduct (thanks society, you REALLY help with this *eye roll*). She lived in an iron lung for a year while her entire family put their lives on hold because they thought they were going to lose their daughter. Causing lots of jealousy, resentment, and attention issues both within my grandmother and between her older sister and her which eventually turned into an all out ostracization of my grandmother from most of her family at the hands of her bitter older sister.

I realized that our relationships with others, our relationships with ourselves, and furthermore our relationships with money are not as simple as they seem. I started to realize my own lack of self worth due to abandonment issues around my father. I also started to unpack resentment towards my mother for not giving me what I needed, a consistent father figure. Which caused me to overcompensate with male energy to balance the household at the times when she was unable. Through all of this, I realized it wasn't her fault and I had to stop subconsciously blaming her. She was doing the best she could, hell she was doing MORE than the best that most people could under the circumstances. She was essentially a superhero.

It also made me realize my grandmother had some of these same tendencies, including resentment towards my mother for getting in the way and resentment towards herself for not pouring into her daughter more. This layering of pain, trauma, and negative emotions came out in low vibrational ways such as petty comments or lashing out. Seeing this behavior at a young age made me feel like it was acceptable, and I used this as a vehicle to fuel my subconscious resentment towards my mother. All of these misunderstood emotions left unchecked began to develop into a form of self hate regarding the part of me who played or felt like the victim.

As we discussed earlier in the trauma cycle, there are numerous protector emotions that form in layers over our trauma. The deepest layer of this protection is often self hate. This is because in our society, it is typically thought of as acceptable or commonplace to complain and cast judgement towards others. So hate projected outwardly is somewhat normalized. Thus we frequently get stuck on this element, causing us to run on a feedback loop in the trauma cycle. We find it much harder to feel this hate inwardly towards ourselves. This self hate is often considered a form of depression or more complex forms of mental health issues. Which sure, we as a society are opening up more and more about. However, we still have a ways to go.

This is why it is so important to do this sort of assessment of your upbringing. To break down and analyze the beliefs and experiences that played a role in shaping your own money story. Because without doing this deep work, you are living a life controlled by your emotions. A life dictated by your trauma. And this will show up in your relationships, it will show up in your health, and it will show up in your finances until you commit to doing the deep work to heal.

And I want to remind you that you are not alone. I know this shit ain't easy. This is hard work. And it is not for the faint of heart. But you are strong. You are a fighter. You are a daughter (or son) of the Utmost High. And I want you to know I am out here with you. I am in the trenches by your side doing the work. Doing the heavy lifting and breaking generational curses. So that you, and your children, and your children's children can live a better life. A life in alignment with your highest calling. So keep doing the work. I see you. I acknowledge you. And I honor you.

CHAPTER 14

FORGIVENESS

You guys have heard about my mom by now. Single mother, hard working, strong values, superhero status, you know the type. I could brag on her all day. She, and the resilience that formed as a byproduct of not having my father around, made me the woman I am today. Over one Thanksgiving holiday I went to Texas to visit family. I spent a few days in Dallas visiting my dad, Austin for a quick getaway with the boo thang, then Padre Island to see my Aunt Shawn. When I got to Dallas, my dad was a mess. The house was a mess, we went out to dinner and that was a mess, the whole thing was a mess. I'm coaching my older brother (same dad, different moms) who is almost 10 years older than me to get his life together because he is so damaged from the trauma my father put him through. It about broke my heart y'all.

That's when I realized something crazy. I was actually glad my dad wasn't a part of my life growing up. I was glad to break the toxic cycle of anger, trauma, alcoholism, and emotional abuse. I spent my whole life wondering why he wasn't around, what was wrong with me, and yet here I was at 26 years old standing looking at the chaos and instability present in their lives thanking God that I chose a different path. That I was able to rise above all of this pain. So I went home with this heavy on my heart.

As I was writing this book, God made it clear to me that I needed to put more of my heart and soul into it if I really want to change some damn lives. If I really want to make an impact and help you to transform your life, I have to show you mine. And not just the healed, transformed, easy to talk about parts. The nitty gritty, the pain, the sorrow, the tears, all of it. I've got to lay it all out there for the world to see to lift others up and show you that they are not alone. You matter. Your story matters. And your story can SAVE LIVES.

One Sunday I was sitting in church service in a movie theater...yep, you read that right...and Pastor Mike was giving a sermon about coming home for Christmas. He was praying on forgiveness and the Holy Spirit just hit me like a ton of bricks and everything became so clear. So allow me to set the stage a bit. A few years prior when I was 23 years old I got really sick while I was studying abroad in London. I was in a new country away from all of my friends and family, feeling very isolated and alone. It was a blessing in disguise though, because I had some serious coming to Jesus moments. This included the realization that I was waiting on an apology that was never going to come from my father regarding his absence in my life.

So I mustered up the courage to reach out to him and start the dialogue. I wanted to get this off my chest and establish some level of closure. So we were messaging on What'sApp (shout out to my international homies, you know what's good) and I told him the truth. I was waiting on an apology that was never going to come. He said there was nothing he could say or do to make it up to me. And that he knows I can probably never forgive him, but that he's sorry and he f*cked up. FYI my dad cusses like a sailor. Maybe that's where I get it from. He also said that he loves me and is so proud of the life I've built (this was like 3 level ups ago, ayeeeee) and he knows I'm going to do great things. Essentially best case scenario considering the circumstances, right?

Well, after visiting that Thanksgiving holiday I realized it wasn't enough. There was still a bit of pain in my heart that was left unhealed. As the prayer about forgiveness started to work deep into my soul, I had an epiphany. A divine appointment to reach out to my father and let him know that I forgive him. Sure, I told him I was waiting on an apology that would never come and we addressed the big elephant in the room. However, I didn't tell him I forgave him. I'm not sure I understood that I needed to, and I'm also not sure if I was even ready for that. After seeing his pain and the emotional instability present in the lives of him and those close to him, I realized I had the ability to grant my father a freedom he needed so deeply. The freedom of forgiveness.

Sure, maybe not every element of my father's life was a byproduct of our relationship or lack thereof. However, there was no denying that guilt and shame played a solid role in the equation. Guilt and shame are two of the lowest vibrational emotions, and it was clear from the low vibe activities that there was some damage, hurt, and trauma being ignored in that household. So the Holy Spirit spoke to me. I mean this more metaphorically than literally for those of you getting freaked out already. C'mon, we've made it through karmic debt, fractures and connected consciousness, you can do this too. Any who, I knew what I needed to do. I needed to reach out to my father and let him know that I forgave him. The following is an excerpt from the letter I wrote to him:

"I forgive you. I forgive you for not being a part of my childhood. I forgive you for not contributing financially as my mother struggled to provide for me. I forgive you for missing volleyball games, dance recitals, and the father-daughter dance in kindergarten. I forgive you for not being at my graduation. I forgive you for forgotten birthdays, missed holidays, and broken promises. I forgive you for leaving me with daddy issues that caused me to put relationships with men above my own self worth for years. I forgive you for showing up for your other two children and leaving me to fend for myself. Most importantly, I forgive you for not being the father that I deserved."

Let me be clear, I didn't say all of this to be petty. I didn't say all of this to hurt his feelings and drive the dagger deeper. I said all of this because it needed to be said. I said all of this because it's what I needed to let go of to be able to honestly forgive him from the bottom of my heart and the dustiest corners of my soul.

So my question to you is, who do you need to forgive? What do you need to reconcile in your heart so that you can begin to let go? Let go of the baggage holding you back from rising to the next level. To create space for something more. A deeper connection with yourself and others. And ultimately, your own alignment and peace. Take a moment to journal around this. Whatever comes up for you, I recommend discussing it with a friend you know you can trust. Ask them to hold you accountable to taking whatever follow up or action you need to open your heart and release forgiveness. You know where to find us if you need additional support!

CHAPTER 15

LETTING GO: RELEASING & CREATING SPACE

The only way to truly let go is to first give the ideas and emotions you feel are holding you back space. Without agreeing or disagreeing, listen to those parts of yourself and honor them. Only then can you unbind your heart and truly start to heal.

This exercise takes A LOT of compassion. In order to fully release the negative emotions you harness and often suppress or repress, you must forgive. And in order to forgive, sometimes in the face of unspeakable atrocities and trauma, you have to understand that it's not their fault. Hear me out. The society that we live in shapes and conditions us with lies of scarcity and whatever other toxic methods necessary to ensure we continue to consume. To drive profits and increase the income gap even more. To lift up the 1% so they can continue to hold power and control. So the fact that we are even here in this place to be putting in the work to heal the trauma and break the cycle is astounding. So let's take a moment to acknowledge you.

Your power.
Your resilience.
Your undeniable strength.

I am so proud of you for standing up for yourself, your family, your legacy by making a choice to break the cycle of pain and hurt so that you can write a different narrative. One where you are the victor, not the victim. The hero, not the oppressed. All because you turned inward and started to do the work on you. So you go, girl!

And once you start to extend this compassion to others, including those who have hurt you then you can start to heal. This is especially important with family and those closest to you if you would like to maintain a healthy relationship. If you hold on to the anger, the resentment, the pain, and allow it to guide your life, you continue to give them control. You continue to give your pain control. Control over your choices, your feelings, and eventually your life. So stop that! Sever the cord of control that the pain has over you. This requires a decision. A decision to no longer allow it to taint your beautiful energetic space and mind. Your heart and soul. I'm not saying this is easy, I'm just saying that it is necessary. In the following pages we are going to continue to discuss tools for you to utilize to release the emotions associated with the personal trauma you've faced. Remember, we are in this together.

CHAPTER 16

SELF LOVE

Self love can be HARD. Especially in a world where women receive messages every single day from the media telling them they are too skinny, too fat, too young, too old, too overbearing, too weak...the list of contradictions goes on and on and on. We are constantly measuring ourselves against this standard and wondering why we can never be enough. So self love and self worth are deeply intertwined. It's no wonder why self love is so damn hard.

However, there is still hope. A courageous group of women have begun a counter cultural movement around self love in the form of self care. And while we are all a work in progress and that is perfectly okay, every single act of self care brings you that much closer to self love. For it is you taking a moment to pour time, love, and energy into YOU. Because you deserve it.

In addition, self care is a critical element of a balanced life. And in this age of overworking and burnout, it's more important than ever. Self care is important for your family and friends too. They learn from you, so setting healthy boundaries to take care of yourself shows them that they too need to put themselves first and not continue to overextend themselves.

For my own self care routine, I make it a ritual. I start by lighting a candle to create an intention of ME time. Nothing else can touch me or come into my space until I seal the practice and blow out the candle. Sometimes I burn sage at first to cleanse the energy and allow me to begin my self care practice on a clean slate. Then close my practice with palo santo at the end to seal with positive energy and bless my day. Other days I begin with prayer and meditation and seal my practice with a mantra or mudra meditation.

Some of my go-tos during this intentional time include yoga, journaling, meditation, prayer, Bible study, worship, spending time with God, hot baths (try epsom salts, bubbles, bath bombs, and face or hair masks if you want to really take it to the next level), quiet time in nature, and beach days, weather permitting.

Taking care of yourself is a key element of alignment. It also is the number one way to avoid burnout. Taking care of yourself can include having a solid skin care routine. It might mean going to the gym or exercising regularly. It could mean going to a dance class once in a while or switching up your workouts if you get bored. Masterbation could also be another form of self care. Yep, I said it.

Self care also doesn't always have to be alone. Maybe it means a girls night or Sex in the City-esq lunch dates. Or if a romantic dinner with your partner or some incredible orgasmic sex is what allows you to honor yourself, unplug, and refuel, THEN GO FOR IT! The world is your oyster. So get creative!

I urge you to tap into you regularly. At first perhaps try once a week. I dedicate Mondays to self care, for example. Once you get comfortable with that, I would begin to implement self care daily. I myself take 1-2 hours of self care time every morning to prime my day. As an entrepreneur, I have that sort of flexibility. If that doesn't work for you and your schedule, try implementing the self care routine at night. The key is that you get into a routine. This consistency is what is going to give you the power to handle life when it throws you the inevitable curveball. This will become your energetic reserve in which you pull from when the shit hits the fan, aka when life happens.

CHAPTER 17

SELF WORTH

For many women, self worth is the biggest roadblock between them and their deepest desires. Is it why you aren't getting what you deserve? What could this lack of self worth be holding you back from?

Asking for that raise? Negotiating a higher salary when you land the position of your dreams? Starting that business? Taking the trip of a lifetime? Landing that dream client? Taking your life and business to the next level?

In order for good things to come your way, you must believe that you deserve them. And not just on the surface. But deep, deep inside. Both energetically and in your subconscious mind, you have to believe you are worthy. Also, while we are here...Why have you always insisted on proving your worth to others and never requested others to prove their worth to you?

My biggest limiting belief in this season has been the LIE that I am not worthy of holding wealth. Who am I to become wealthy? Who am I to be rich? Well, let me tell you who I am. I am Lindsay Lucianna Lawless. I am a daughter of a King and that makes me royalty. I am a lover, a fighter, a healer, an author, community leader, business owner, sister, prayer warrior, a friend...should I keep going? I am powerful in my own right. And let me tell you something. So are you.

I want you to write a love letter to yourself, similar to the proclamation I just made. I want you to tell me, no tell YOURSELF what makes you great. What makes you worthy. Because at the end of the day it's not about what your cousin thinks about you, what your neighbor thinks about you, or what your co-worker thinks about you. It's about what YOU think of you that's going to make all the difference.

You bring that energy into everything you do. How you feel about you determines how you show up in the world. I also want to give a brief disclaimer about the differences between worthiness and confidence. For most of my life I was (and am) very confident. I believed in myself and my abilities. I believed in my ability to navigate a room, meet new people, and be the center of attention. But what happened as I got older is that I confused this with self worth. I thought, nah, I'm good in that department. I don't need to work on that. When in reality, my lack of self worth was affecting EVERYTHING.

So for those rare unicorns that came out of the womb with unshakable confidence ready to take on the world, don't get it twisted. Confidence and worth are not interchangeable. Once I had this breakthrough and started to do the deep work on my self worth, my entire life changed. I leveled up my relationships. I no longer allowed people to use me or put myself in situations that compromised my integrity. I also let go of a lot of guilt that surrounded my ideas of leveling up. "I don't want them to think I think I'm better than them. I don't want to feel like I'm leaving anyone behind." And all of these other thoughts and fears that came creeping up on me when I was focused on confidence alone. Confidence is the light that will draw people to you. Self worth is the discernment that will keep the wrong from sucking your energy, like a pesky mosquito.

If you are wanting to integrate some energy work into healing your relationship with yourself and leveling up your self worth, look to the womb. The incubator for life itself. The sacral chakra. Also known in Sanskrit as Svadhisthana chakra, this energetic center controls your body's ability to regulate emotions, tap into your creativity and sexuality, and honor yourself. It is located above the pubic bone and below the navel. The sacral chakra affects creativity, confidence, and worthiness in relation to yourself. If this chakra is out of balance, it can also show up in your relationship with money. It may result in feeling unworthy of holding wealth, something I've experienced & talked about time and time again. It may show up as you feeling unworthy of raising your prices or unworthy of landing that raise. Perhaps you feel unworthy of getting the support you need, creating boundaries, or asking for help.

As we go through our lives and get older, we are too often discouraged from creative expression. When you're a kid, it's socially acceptable to play pretend, use your imagination, color outside of the lines, and just be you. However, as we get older we often feel the pressure to get serious. To conform to societal norms, follow the rules, and grow up. To color between the lines, stop playing around, and quit daydreaming.

So if you are looking to open up your sacral chakra, you must engage in some not so serious play time. Do you remember what it was like to play as a kid? If these memories are challenging for you to tap into, try watching your children or nieces & nephews, play. Then begin to play as if you have nothing to lose. No fear of failure or judgement. This could be through cooking, gardening, starting a new project, painting, coloring, building a sandcastle, you name it. Play is the single handed best exercise for tapping into our creativity and balancing our second chakra.

It is the color orange, and the mantra that corresponds to the Svadhisthana chakra is the sound VAM. By chanting or repeating this mantra, your vibrations will open up and align the sacral chakra. The gemstones for this chakra are amber, calcite orange, carnelian, & hematite also. There are also tons of meditations and yoga sequences to support the balancing of this chakra. More on this in the resources section at the end of Part II.

A balanced second chakra leads to feelings of wellness, abundance, pleasure, and joy. When this chakra is out of balance, a person may experience emotional instability, fear of change, sexual dysfunction, depression, or addictions. You can open this chakra with creative expression and by honoring your body. The energy of this chakra is feminine, passive, and lunar.

Now that you have an understanding of your energetic center when it comes to self worth, let's talk for a second about limiting beliefs. In my own money story, I realized that while I didn't actually hold negative beliefs around money or rich people, I had normalized poverty. Being poor was normal to me, and thus it was okay to continue doing and being what I thought was normal. So let me say, IT'S NOT F*CKING NORMAL. It is not normal to go without. It's not normal to move in with your mom's friend because you can't afford to keep the lights on, and it's not normal for your grandmother to hold it over your mom's head when she needs a little extra support. NONE of these things are normal. And if they are for you, let me go ahead and come out and say it: they shouldn't be.

It is our divine right to live a life that lights us up. To be and feel fully supported. It's not a privilege. It's not something only afforded to the few. It is your birthright. Regardless of what other schools of thought, or the enemy may want you to believe, you were not put on this planet just to suffer and die. You were put on this planet to live. To THRIVE.

CHAPTER 18

PLAYING SMALL

There is some need you are serving that is holding you back from creating the abundance you know you are capable of. We all do it at some point or another. Is it your ego? Unwilling to take a few steps back to catapult yourself forward? Is it friends or family talking down on or not taking seriously your great ideas? Do people you care about look negatively on wealthy people? Is it a fear of your own greatness? A fear of responsibility?

Whatever it is for you, you need to get crystal clear about it so you can start to work to overcome it. Take a few moments to journal about what is holding you back from taking your life, and thus your relationship with money, to the next level.

While you reflect on that, let's talk about responsibility. Often people are playing small to avoid responsibility. Here's the thing though. As conscious adults, we all have responsibilities. There's no getting out of it. You have a responsibility to provide for yourself. Maybe you have a responsibility to provide for your parents and other family members. If you are a parent you have a responsibility to provide for your children. The list goes on and on. Avoiding these responsibilities doesn't make them go away. Making less money and playing small doesn't make them go away.

Making more money and stepping into your true power on the other hand makes you MORE capable of providing for yourself, your family, and ultimately taking care of your responsibilities. Once you embark on this journey to heal your money trauma, things begin to change. You start to do the tough work and little by little, it begins to show. You start to feel a freedom and independence welling up inside of you. Before you know it, the frequency of abundance doesn't feel so far away anymore.

Imagine this: You see an opportunity at work you may have thought you weren't qualified for before and now you decide you're going to start playing bigger. You take on the project, do extremely well, and before long you land a promotion. Or maybe you decide to pursue a client that you've dreamed of working with but thought you couldn't work with because they're a "bigger fish." You land this client and finally start getting paid the rates you deserve. Before you know it, this greatness starts to snowball. Your kids see this boldness and tenacity and they start to become inspired to dream bigger. Your significant other sees the work you are putting in and decides they want to join you on this journey. Not only does your support network grow, but also you begin to be a beacon of light and hope, motivating those around you to their own greatness.

So let me ask you, who or what is it serving by playing small?

CHAPTER 19

YOUR SPIRITUAL & EMOTIONAL TOOLKIT

1. **Your Money Story** – To help you understand your money story, do the following exercises:

   What was your parent's relationship with money like growing up? Journal around this and then pick out the most important 3-5 themes.

Identify the core memories or the first time you recall these themes being present.

Start to think about specific phrases or words that they used that illustrated these underlying themes. For example, if you were raised by a single mother, you may have noticed a theme of scarcity and never having enough. This may have manifested in communication such as "we can't afford that."

Write down all of the negative thoughts and phrases that come to mind.

Then rewrite them in a way that supports you, using the framework we discussed in the Journaling section of Chapter 5: Tools for Shifting Your Mindset at the end of Part I. In the example above, that may look like reframing to "we have the resources we need."

2. **Affirmations** - Below are some examples I've utilized in my own healing journey. You should also write out some specific ones as discussed above.

Pick 3-5 affirmations that resonate most with you, write them out regularly, and keep them in a place where you can see them every day.

I am a money magnet.
I am wealthy.
I can afford that.
I have the resources I need.
I can do anything I set my mind to.
I am whole.
I am abundant.
I love money and money loves me.
Money is important. It supports my mission & life's work.
You have to work smart to create sustainable wealth.
Money quite literally grows on trees.
Money has the value I assign to it.
There is more than enough money to go around.
There are so many ways to make money.

I can make money doing what I love and what lights me up.

More money equals more freedom.

I use my money as a conduit for my highest commitments.

I make making money fun.

Money is all around me and completely within reach.

I deserve to be appropriately compensated.

I don't need a backup plan, because I trust God & I trust myself.

Those who truly love me will be there no matter what my position.

Take the ones you need and leave the rest. Be sure to also write your own affirmations depending on your unique money story and needs. Remember, this framework for healing is all about integration with the goal of alignment. Once you are in alignment, I recommend only revisiting things as they come up from time to time. Otherwise, you may keep yourself stuck in a perpetual trauma cycle of pain. And that is NOT the goal! You deserve better than that.

3. If you are looking to plug into a spiritual community to deepen your relationship with God, check out the V1 Podcast available on iTunes, Spotify, YouTube, and pretty much every social platform. Connecting to V1 has accelerated my spiritual growth in so many ways and I can't thank them enough for the discipleship my husband and I have received from their leadership.

4. Journey Junkie has a ton of amazing yoga and meditation videos on YouTube with more of a spiritual and healing component. Her videos and her community have been an integral part of my self-care routine for years. My first classes with her were a chakra yoga 7 day challenge and these helped to set the tone for what would become a two hour long ritual of priming my day every morning. I highly recommend her Body Mind Soul Studio as well if you are looking for higher level training.

5. Teal Swan is a spiritual thought leader with trainings and resources on healing, emotions, childhood trauma, and other topics we've touched on. If you're interested in learning more about any of that, check her out. She goes deep into all of these topics and more on her YouTube channel.

PART III:

TRANSFORMATIONAL MONEY STORIES FROM EXTRAORDINARY WOMEN LIKE YOU

CHAPTER 20

CASE STUDIES & PERSONAL STORIES FROM WOMEN

We asked a few women to share their money stories, including how they overcame adversity, broke generational curses, went from poverty to prosperity, and so much more. We incorporated a few open ended questions to get them on the right track as well as encourage them to go deep and get vulnerable. The answers we received were profound. There were so many connections, even though none of these women had even met. Our hope is that these stories from ordinarily extraordinary women just like you will inspire you. That they will light a fire under your ass to get ready to take some serious action. And to show you that it's possible for you too.

You can create your very own money success story.

CHAPTER 21

THE POWERFUL
MATRIARCH

Lysa Lawless is a Certified Paralegal on the path to a new and financially independent version of herself. She is also my best friend, my confidant, my rock, my very own superhero, and most importantly, my mother. I'm also honored to be her Money Consciousness Coach. Before working together, Lysa felt uncertain, fearful, unworthy, insecure, and avoidant about money. While we've only been working together for a few weeks, she now feels motivated and like force of nature gaining momentum in her relationship with money.

LYSA'S MONEY STORY:

Regarding my values around money, I have always been dependent on a physical employer and tied up my value as a "worker bee" in approval and financial reward from a third party. While there is absolutely nothing wrong with being a "worker bee", for me I felt held down or submissive more than I felt empowered and enriched. Money matters to me as it's a way to feel autonomous and in control of my life. I want to feel financially independent and self-reliant, which is why I am beginning a new path for my life and my future.

Mindset is everything. When you don't have the proper mindset, you don't even realize that it is the most important thing. It can propel you forward or hold you back in your life. If your mindset is one of defeat, you will be defeated. If your mindset is powerful, you will be powerful. At a few points in my life I have felt that power within me, but I have been too afraid of taking risks, mostly due to being a single mother. There was more at risk that just my welfare. In my generation, women were taught to stay in a box. I was taught how to be a wife and a mother, but not how to be my fully independent self. So I was too afraid to step outside of that. I always saw the downsides of taking risks, not the upsides.

Becoming my true, empowered self is the most important thing to me now. Changing and strengthening my mindset are tantamount to experiencing and enjoying the future I want to see in my life. I am becoming the person I have always wanted to be. While I'm still in the early days of going through the program, I feel more in control of my life. My mindset is evolving in the direction I want it to go and grow. I KNOW what I am capable of. Now I simply need guidance to organize my path, gather my strength, and build the foundation on which my future will thrive, which is exactly what the Heal Money Trauma & Create Sustainable Wealth Program provides.

Working with Lindsay, one of the first topics we dove into was how my parents related to money growing up. They never discussed money, or finances, or gave me a realistic view of the importance of money. Money was a big secret when I was growing up. There were no lessons on budgeting and the importance of planning for daily living or the future. They showed through their actions how you spend it, but not what it takes to get there. This left me feeling uncertain around money. It also made me feel like I couldn't be trusted with this privy information and like I didn't deserve to know how much money my parents made.

Since unpacking that, I have identified some pivotal moments that shaped my relationship with money. This childhood trauma, though I didn't see it that way at the time, caused me to avoid my finances for years. It made me feel unworthy of receiving money and insecure around managing it. Before I began this journey, I was fearful and uncertain. I lived from a place of necessity and scarcity. Now I feel my self confidence growing. I am empowered and taking charge of monumental to do lists in multiple aspects of my life.

Last year my mother passed away and I inherited her estate and everything she left behind. This included property, investment accounts, and all of her belongings from a lifetime of travels, borderline hoarding. Ensuring I am able to leave a legacy behind for my children is something that's incredibly important to me. I also don't want to leave them with the same burdens. This is something that requires a whole new mindset and skill set. Through the support of my daughter, I am beginning to trust myself to navigate this brave new world.

I am also taking time to allow myself to feel a sense of accomplishment at each milestone. Yes, some days I have to remind myself that I am in charge and that I have accomplished something. That I can and will continue to grow. Whenever I start to feel uncertain, I stop and remind myself to look at what I have accomplished so far. To acknowledge how much closer I am every day to my goals. Lindsay created a spreadsheet to help me prioritize tasks and the first tab includes everything I've crossed off and all of the wins I've already accomplished. Every day brings me closer to being the master of my destiny.

While I am still early on in this journey, I know that forgiveness and letting go will play the largest role in healing my money trauma. I have to let go of past behavior regarding money, living by scarcity and fear, and remaining apathetic to my financial future. I can and I will master my relationship with money.

I also think all of us link our self worth to money in one way or another. Either through the job we hold, the degrees we have, the socio-economic set we align with, where we live, or what we wear or drive. I have always known the value of my "self", even when I could see how I was misperceived through another's eyes. I knew they were wrong if they judged me as inferior. I really never thought myself lesser than anyone in regard to money. Being an educated, well spoken and loyal individual was always more important to me than money. I would have done well as an academic in that regard.

The truth of my inner self, however, knows that money is power. That is literally what I was told as a youth and I see clearly how that is applied in daily living. However, while money may bring you power, being in control of your financial self and future is the most empowering.

Lysa Lawless, a former Paralegal with experience in small business management, sales and advertising, currently runs a growing short term rental business. Drawing on her experience from sales and design for a national interior wholesale company as well as business development, she consults potential and existing short term rental owners on interior design and marketing on platforms such as Airbnb, VRBO and Home Away.

Website: www.the5ivesenses.com

CHAPTER 22

THE GREEN GODDESS

Valeria Hernández is a former engineer turned plant-based health coach. She's a first generation Mexican-American who grew up in Southern California, Mexico, Atlanta and probably came out of the womb wanting to save the world! Ever since she could remember, she had a passion for wanting to help people, the earth, and animals. She's now aware this stems from her empathic tendencies. I've had the pleasure of working with Valeria, coaching her around her money and business. Before working together, she felt uncertain, unworthy, insecure, avoidant, and guilty in her relationship with money. Watching her grow has been such an honor. In a few short months she has already created systems to scale her business, tripled her income, and transformed her relationship with money.

VALERIA'S MONEY STORY:

Growing up I was an achievement addict. Being the best, getting straight A's, and being liked by my teachers was a rush. This behavior combined with my love for sustainability and nature lead me to study environmental engineering in college. I made lots of decisions in college solely based on the questions of "will this help me make more money?" or "will this help me get more scholarships?" instead of unapologetically following my TRUE passion, the intersection of climate change and animal agriculture. Turns out, the universe has a funny way of always aligning us with our true calling if we chose to let it guide us. Which has led me to where I am now: a Plant-Based Health & Wellness Coach helping women eat more plants, fall in love with their bodies & themselves, and step into their true bad-assery.

My core values are justice, authenticity, freedom, and compassion. I truly believe for something to be in alignment and worth selling it needs to be a win-win-win. This is something I originally heard from Kyle Cease that REALLY resonated with me. It needs to be a win for me, a win for my clients or the end consumer, and a win for the earth and society at large. If one of these three things are missing it feels inauthentic to me. Which is why plant-based, compassionate living is at the very core of everything I do.

Authenticity and freedom are two values I've always had idealistically but didn't start truly embodying until recently. Most of my life I've been trying to fit a mold of who I think I should be instead of embracing that I am enough as I am. Right here and now. Constantly reminding myself of that and repeating the mantra "I am enough" is one of the most freeing things I've experienced. Especially as a Latina, when messages all around me including society, politicians, and even school counselors have told me that I'm not enough.

As a recovering achievement addict along with these mixed signals I received, I created a bad habit of tying my worth to numbers. Money is no exception. I used to think my self worth was tied to my net worth and to be honest still sometimes slip into that negative headspace. The difference is now I bounce back from that way faster whereas in the past I would wallow in self pity thinking of all my debts. Through working with Lindsay, I have the tools to remind myself that my worth is not tied to any number. Not my GPA, not my weight, not my body fat percentage, not my cash flow, nor my annual income. My self worth is immeasurable because I'm effin priceless.

Money matters to me because it lets me invest more towards justice and compassion, particularly through giving back to non-profits in the areas of social justice and food empowerment. It lets me be more ME and more authentic in addition to giving me the freedom to live life on my terms, be my own boss, and expand as much as I want. Money matters to me because it's given me and my family countless opportunities. It has allowed us to seek better, more fulfilled lives and generally speaking, it's the root of a lot of awesome in the world!

Mindset is EVERYTHING when it comes to money. Mindset is everything when it comes to life. It drives our actions, our habits, our behaviors, and our beliefs. You can have all the fanciest budget trackers, business strategies, and money-making tools but without the right mindset they ain't worth shit.

Ever since I can remember, my mom has had an abundant mindset when it came to money. She had no qualms when it comes to spending but wouldn't be reckless with money. She always reminded me if there's any area of life you should always invest in, it's yourself. My biological dad on the other hand has always had a strained relationship with money. He complains that he can't "make it" as a musician and that money is the root of all evil. He has a victim mentality with money and shys away from income-generating opportunities. My second dad, who I grew up with from ages 5 to 25, had a generally healthy relationship with money. I never remember him complaining about it. However, as I left behind my traditional 9-5 engineering job to kickstart my entrepreneurial career, I noticed a lot of confusion from his end on how I was making money and if I had enough stability.

I feel like this confusion or uncertainty may have rubbed off on me to a degree. For the longest time I thought there was some secret that all the 6 and 7 figure earners of the world had that I didn't. A special sauce or something that they were keeping to themselves and only sharing with their clients. This made me feel like I wasn't worthy without a certain course or mastermind. Since then, my mindset has shifted into realizing that there is no secret. I have everything I need to be absurdly wealthy inside of me. As a result of my experience healing money trauma, I now know that abundance is not something external that I get from somewhere else, it's something I embody and open myself to receiving.

Forgiveness and letting go also played a huge role in healing. They honestly continue to play a role. The more I explore the deep, deep money memories I have, the more I find myself needing to forgive people, experiences, and mainly my past selves. Letting go of my fears has been key because at the end of the day, the worst case scenario isn't even that bad in the grand scheme of life. The release I've experienced as a result of letting go is what gives SPACE for abundance to come.

I used to think rich people were greedy, talking about money was tacky, and that to make money I needed to work all day every day. I now KNOW that all those things are not only false but also hurtful to my relationship with money. How would money ever come to me if I had all these negative thoughts about it all day long? What you focus on grows. So by shifting the money stories I've been telling myself, reframing these limiting beliefs and raising my vibration to that of abundance I've been able to truly step into my power as an entrepreneur and business owner. I've always known deep down I'm meant for more in life. I've been called to fulfill this huge mission in the world, but sometimes I used to think it was just a silly dream. Now I know it's so much more than a hope, it's a reality. As a result, it is my duty to heal my money lies and become massively wealthy for the good of all the causes and people I want to serve.

I am so grateful for the opportunity to heal and the commitment to my growth. I now feel confident, empowered, motivated about money. Working with Lindsay has been instrumental in this transformation. She is the perfect balance of patience and tough love! She's not afraid to tell clients what they NEED to hear even if it's not what they WANT to hear. And she actually holds you accountable to taking action and is super organized in tracking your progress and having you take ownership. If your intuition has led you here and you're thinking about working with Lindsay then DO IT! She's one of the best coaches I've worked with.

I'd also like to share one of my key life hacks. Remembering that health is also a form of wealth. Without it you can't truly enjoy your massive financial abundance. Always take care of your body & mind first. Once you're in alignment, the money will follow!

Valeria is a passionate Plant-Based Health Coach dedicated to helping women
go from exhausted to ENERGIZED AF by eating more plants, staying accountable to their fitness & nutrition, and tuning into their inner badass. You can find her hanging on the Gram @vegivale or check out her Facebook page VegiVale if you want to stay connected with her, talk to her about wellness coaching, or learn more about leading a vegan lifestyle.

Website: www.vegivale.com

CHAPTER 23

THE DEBT FREE NURSE

Allie Grotteland is an RN studying to be a Nurse Practitioner. I met Allie at Rachel Luna's live event Confidence Activated in Atlanta, Georgia and had the privilege of working alongside her in a following Mastermind. She has incredible energy, a strong sense of community, and is a total go getter! She recently paid off 36k of student loan and credit card debt in one year. Say whattt?! Since then she has made it her mission to create a safe space for nurses to talk finances so they can demolish debt and save without sacrifice.

ALLIE'S MONEY STORY:

How I currently feel about money: abundant, empowered, smart, and motivated.

I value time, traveling, spending time with my family and retiring early. In terms of how I relate to money, I see money as freedom! I no longer want to have debt because it limits my choices for careers, lifestyle and what I want to do in life.

Mindset is very important when it comes to money. When I am in the right mindset and choose to focus on abundance instead of lack I am more successful with managing my money. I used to believe I would never have enough money. I would spend all of it and wasn't good at saving. I also had a lot of debt. I thought I would always be in debt and that managing my money would never be something I was good at. I finally decided I didn't want to live like that anymore and made a commitment to take control of my money.

Growing up, my mom hid a lot of her money from us. We were taught it was rude to ask people how much they made. My mom never told us about how much she saved, what she did with her money, or why she worked so much. She would work a lot of extra shifts to afford the things we wanted and needed.

A lot has changed since then. I now believe that money is fluid. I work extra shifts when I want to, not because I have to. I know that I deserve all the abundance. Money comes to me easily. And I am able to manage it better.

Before I chose to change my money story, my self worth was tied to my debt and my lack of money. Now my self worth has nothing to do with my debt or the amount of money I have. During this transformation, I also had to extend myself a lot of compassion. I had to forgive myself for being a poor steward of my own money and for making mistakes.

Allie is a Nurse and a money coach for nurses. Since paying off 36K in debt in one year, she is on her way to becoming completely debt free over the next few months. She helps nurses demolish debt and save without sacrifice. Feel free to connect with her on social media at The_debtfreenurse if you are a nurse looking to lean into and grow with an amazing community of like minded women.

Website: www.savingwithoutsacrifice.com

CHAPTER 24

THE ABUNDANT SOULPRENEUR

Angel Quintana is the Founder of Holistic Fashionista Magazine and Mystery School. She is dedicated to supporting Soulpreneurs to discover their divinity, be of service to their Kismet clients®, and help raise the frequency of the planet. I met Angel a few years ago at a time when I was beginning my own exploration and healing journey to reconnect with my soul. Through her teachings, I was able to manifest the business of my dreams and align with my true calling. She also served an instrumental role in helping this book come together as I attended her 3 Day Author Symposium back in January of 2019. During this training Angel provided the tools I needed to hone my message, self publish, and market *Heal Money Trauma & Create Sustainable Wealth* effectively. I am immensely grateful for her beautiful soul and the work she is doing to support women leaders around the globe.

ANGEL'S MONEY STORY:

To be honest, money isn't something I spend much time thinking or worrying about. I value money in the sense that I don't waste money. Because money is energy, being wasteful with regards to money is to be wasteful with my energy. I feel very abundant about money.

That hasn't always been the case though. When I had no money and severe credit card debt, it was a direct reflection of how I spent my time and energy. It was also a reflection of self worth at the time. Improving my self worth got me out of debt. I know that to be in debt is merely a reflection of an Inner game, one that is not played very well. Once I realized money was a direct reflection of how I felt about myself and how wasteful I was with my energy, I easily and quickly was able to pay off all my debt.

Money is just a concept we created and its lesson is to share with you at what frequency you're vibrating. I value how I feel, therefore the value of money is only a mirror of that worth. These reflections are essential communications and signs from the Universe.

Regarding how my parents related to money growing up, my mother was a single mom of three children. She was always working and constantly said things like, "I can't afford that." Although she was responsible with money, such as paying her bills on time, she wasn't in a vibrational alignment to wealth or financial freedom; and therefore never had it. This is an ancestral karmic cycle I am honored to break.

The mind is a powerful tool in having as little or as much money as you believe you can have. However, I found that becoming consumed by the concept of money or constantly thinking and strategizing around how to make more of it only takes into consideration the masculine principles of being financially abundant. Money isn't important to me, but my ability to trust the Universe in supplying me with all the resources and opportunities I need to be prosperous absolutely is! I never run out of ideas to pursue my passion, but money is never a factor in whether I embark on those ideas or not. If the idea of passion feels good, I do it. I just do what I love and as cliché as it sounds, I always have enough. It's only when I obsessed, which is never anymore, that money became scarce.

I used to be a workaholic and I made a ton of money. Turns out, I know first hand that money doesn't buy happiness; it just made me want more money, which was actually useless! Chasing money and the fruits of what it can buy me is not a goal of mine any longer because I already know that things, houses, shoes, and vacations are only temporary highs. Chasing a temporary high is a low vibration. Following your passions is a high vibration and its rewards are long lasting.

Before transforming my relationship with money, I was in severe credit card debt after running a business that I thought was my life purpose. Once I closed the business, I became very ill and my finances were an incredible mess. It wasn't until I started to do the deep inner healing work that I was able to fully align with my soul's purpose. I then created Holistic Fashionista, a community-based platform for the holistic leaders of tomorrow. Because we know the awakening process can be messy, we provide rituals + resources to support your upgrade from 3D to 5D and help you get your message out to the world.

Angel is a Higher Calling Tarot + Astrology Reader, Intuitive Business Guide, and 5D Practitioner. With extensive astrology and metaphysical self-study, 20+ years experience in building online businesses, and having mentored thousands of holistic leaders around the globe, Angel built a beautiful platform that showcases Soulpreneurs and their high vibrational work + expertise for those seeking wisdom and mindful solutions to their every day problems.

Since her dark night of the soul in 1997 which lasted nearly 20 years, and through a spiritual awakening in 2016, Angel is an educator on an array of topics around: The Age of Aquarius, Soul Astrology, and the Rainbow Bridge. The divine downloads she's received from alchemist St. Germain, eye-opening dream-stories, hypnosis + past life regression, along with numerous healing experiences, has nurtured her connection to the 5th Dimensional Realm, which has provided the foundation for her mystical inner-standings and sacred teachings she shares openly inside the Holistic Fashionista Mystery School.

Angel is also a Certified Holistic Health Practitioner + Nutritional Consultant, apothecary, and a practicing astrologer of 30 years. She is from Encinitas, California and currently resides in the beautiful San Diego neighborhood of Mission Hills where she works from home with her 2 dogs, Phoenix and Bandit. Angel provides Higher Calling readings on YouTube/iTunes and via video conference for those ready to be the change they wish to see in the world.

Website: https://www.holisticfashionista.com/

Social platforms: Holistic Fashionista

CHAPTER 25

THE DAUGHTER OF OVERFLOW

Kiele Hauser is a life consultant specializing in Christian spiritual development. She requires extreme adventure, enjoys taking risks, and loves doing new things. I met Kiele at our church shortly after my husband and I discovered V1. From the moment I met her I knew she was destined for greatness. I was eager to lean in to learn from, grow with, and build a deep relationship with such a strong woman of faith. She is a rockstar, from leading worship to delivering a powerful sermon. Heck, even crying and praying with you after service! Kiele sets the tone for a high level of excellence and devout servant leadership at V1 Church and in her own business.

KEILE'S MONEY STORY:

Money, in and of itself, is neutral. It's neither good or bad. Our perspective around it is what gives it its charge. I believe our ability to use money to leverage our dreams and goals is essential in being able to create maximum impact on the world around us. For me, money is a resource for freedom, success, and influence.

Growing up I lived in a lot of fear. The way my parents related to money strongly affected my own relationship with money. Both of my parents had a great deal of fear around money. They made me feel a lot of shame for liking nice things and wanting to create freedom around money. I felt their fear and adopted it for a long time. However, working through that fear has opened me up to who I was always meant to be.

My mindset around money is so essential to my health as a business owner and life coach. Without the ability to relate healthily to money, I never would have been able to become a successful entrepreneur. It plays into everything, especially in business.

Through dealing with childhood roots and exposing the fear around money, I was able to grow in my worth and confidence. This healing was so important to my success in life and business. I now believe I am worth being compensated the way I deserve. I also have a firm belief that there will always be enough.

I used to live in fear that there wouldn't be enough and that I would never be enough to make enough money. I felt scarce, uncertain, unworthy, and insecure around money. I thought I was on my own, always in survival mode. I didn't understand that God was my provider. When I learned that God was a good father, I was able to rest in the confidence that good fathers always create opportunity for their children to be provided for and protected. It was then that I was able to shift out of fear and into confidence and peace.

Forgiveness and being able to let go played a huge role in my healing process around money. Especially towards my own father, who still struggles with many fears around money and success. I can now hold space for him and his emotions without blaming him for it. He was just trying to protect me.

I used to believe most of my self worth came from how much money I made. I was worried about how good my credit was and what people would think. I was prideful because I had always been able to make plenty of money, even as a teen. It was when I had to learn to live on less that I discovered that I'd falsely built my identity on my ability to make money. So when I didn't have money, I couldn't feel good. Once I made a shift and found my identity through Christ, I was able to heal. I began to have a healthy relationship with money. Now I feel motivated, confident, empowered, and abundant about money.

Kiele is a life strategist for high performers who want to level up their leadership. Using a personalized approach, she reaches deep within her clients to uncover what's slowing them down so they can unlock their full potential through Christ. Feel free to connect with her on Instagram @kielehauser

Website: Kielehauser.com

CHAPTER 26

HENRY-ETTAs

You may have heard of the millennial term HENRYs. If not, let me enlighten you. HENRY is an acronym that stands for High Earners Not Rich Yet. So, staying true to my desire to support gender equality, I felt like HENRY was a lacking a feminine touch. So I coined the term HENRY-ETTAs to give us women a much needed foothold in finance. And also to remind you that life and our relationship with money is about more than just earnings. It stands for High Earners Not Rich Yet - Establishing Their True Assets. Because us Boss Women know that wealth is about so much more than just material possessions. Our true assets are far greater than money, though cash flow is a nice perk too.

That's exactly it though. When you build a solid foundation and align with your core values, money becomes the icing on the cake. However, when you are operating outside of alignment, you continue to chase money. You chase money trying to fill a void. When in reality what you want is happiness, fulfillment, connection, and to feel in love with your life. To wake up every morning filled with passion and curiosity to pursue what lies ahead. All of which comes with an inner peace that money can't buy.

Sounds amazing, right? Well, it's not just a fairytale or "someone else's" life. It's entirely possible for you too. And I know because I've been there. I started from the bottom and worked my way up to building the fulfilling life I now lead. I've felt depressed, anxious, jaded, and tired of life. Like nothing was going to go my way and I was going to be stuck in a funk and poverty forever. People used to tell me I had a dark cloud over me and that trouble just seemed to chase me wherever I went. And you know what I realized?

That dark cloud was a reflection of my pain. It was a byproduct of my unhealed trauma.

I can't speak for everyone, but for me and for many of the women who shared their stories in this book, unhealed trauma was the reason they were living in fear. The reason that they felt depressed, anxious, and even hopeless. I've even manifested physical illnesses and ailments as a result of underlying issues that went unresolved. So let this be a testament to how powerful this work really is. This healing journey is about so much more than just your money. It's about your life, your calling, and your purpose. It's about stepping into your destiny and becoming the best version of yourself.

The tools in this book will help you do just that. They will help you to heal your money trauma and build a solid foundation for your life. One that aligns with your higher calling and empowers you to step into your greatness. It is such an honor to be doing this work alongside you and sharing all of this wisdom with you so that you can heal and achieve fullness. Because at the end of the day, life is about so much more than money. It's about establishing your true assets and aligning with your soul's purpose.

Heal Money Trauma & Create Sustainable Wealth is all about taking an integrative approach to create a lasting transformation. I spent years observing my clients behavior and wondering why the financial tools we applied weren't sustainable. I finally realized it was because of unhealed trauma in their relationship with money. So now that you have done the deep work and begun the process of inner healing, my fellow HENRY-ETTAs, you are ready to dive into the strategy. Join me in creating your very own step-by-step roadmap to sustainable wealth.

PART IV

THE STRATEGY: BUILD YOUR MONEY SUCCESS STORY

CHAPTER 27

CONCLUSIONS & ACTION ITEMS TO BUILD YOUR VERY OWN FINANCIAL ROADMAP

Now that you have done some digging into your relationships with money and heard some success stories from others who have turned their money situation around, it's time to create your own money success story.

In the following section, we will discuss the specific steps and strategies you can take to create sustainable wealth to build a legacy for you and your family.

STATS

1. Women retire with 2/3 of the amount of money as men.
2. Women value downside protection SEVEN TIMES as much as upside.
3. Women keep 71% of their money in cash (which is WAY more than men).
4. Women's salaries peak at 40 while men's salaries peak at 55.
5. Because of the gender pay gap, assuming both invest the same, women will have about $320,000 less then when they retire at 67... meaning her money could last 6 years less than his, even though she's likely to live 3-5 years longer.
6. Yes, you should totally ask for the raise. But did you know investing now can actually have a bigger

impact on your financial future than boosting your salary by 30%?! Now imagine if you do BOTH.[viii]

7. Only 7% of women sit in decision making roles at investment funds.

8. Only 5% of women are being invested in.[ix]

CHAPTER 28

PAY YOURSELF FIRST

Every single time you get paid, you should know how much goes to YOU. Not to Chase, or Capital One, or Student Loans...to you. And once you have an understanding of what that number is - or better yet, what you want that number to be - then you do it FIRST. Before you pay your rent or credit cards or anything else. You have to **pay yourself first.**

Set this up as an auto draft to a savings account which is designated for these funds. When we don't pay ourselves first, we often don't get paid at all. We pay everyone and everything else. We make additional spur of the moment, often emotionally fueled, purchases on clothes, food, or going out and when it comes down to it we barely have enough to coast by until the next paycheck. But not you. You're smarter than that. You have dreams and goals and a vision for your life. So make your vision a reality, and pay yourself first.

I'm going to say this again because I think it's that important: **automation** is key. When you are playing smart and paying yourself first, automate it. When you are building your cash stronghold, automate it. When you are saving for your dream home or to start your own business, automate it. Are you noticing the theme here? Automation is everything. We as people tend to make financial decisions from an emotional place. Oh, I'll do that if I feel like it. I'll buy that or save this if I feel like it. Stop that! You are smarter than that. And you deserve better than that. Automation is how you take the feeling, emotion, and inconsistency out of your finances. It no longer happens when you remember, it happens every single pay period without a second glance or thought. THIS is how you become a master of your finances.

CHAPTER 29

CREATING A CASH STRONGHOLD

What is a cash stronghold and why do you need one? Also referred to as an emergency fund, a cash stronghold is money that you set aside to cover your expenses, anticipated or otherwise. I prefer the cash stronghold language because it sounds much more empowering. It gives you the ability to use these funds not only for a worst case scenario, but also for opportunities. This could mean preparing for life changes such as having kids, quitting your full time job, starting your own biz, or whatever else your heart desires. It can also allow you to cover an unexpected car expense or losing your income for a period of time due to an injury or illness if necessary.

I recommend setting aside a MINIMUM of 3 months' worth of expenses. This can be increased depending on your unique circumstances and your comfort level. How much money do you need to have set aside to feel safe no matter what life throws at you? If it's more than 3 months' worth of expenses, make that number your goal and start saving for it.

There are also certain situations that require a different level of preparation. For example, if you are planning to quit your job, how much money do you need to bring in to replace that income? Bear in mind it's also going to take a bit of time to gain momentum and generate income in your business. How many clients does that translate to? How many hours is it going to take you to manage that client load?

Now take all those numbers and increase them by 10% for "Murphy's Law" - aka shit happens and nothing goes exactly as planned - AND THAT'S OKAY. This is the new normal as an entrepreneur. Hours, increase by 10%, revenue you need to generate because, spoiler alert, you now pay employment tax (employer & employee effectively "split" taxes - now your covering 100% because you are both). Increase by 10% how many clients you think you need. ALL OF IT. You'll thank me later.

CHAPTER 30

ADDITIONAL STREAMS OF INCOME

Let me just go ahead and clear the air about one of the most misunderstood elements of personal & business finances: there is no such thing as truly passive income. I'm going to let that sink in for a minute. If you are one of the people who picked up this book hoping to learn how to get rich quick, this isn't the book for you. And honestly, any one promising that is likely misleading you.

Generating income takes effort. Making additional streams of income takes work. Creating sustainable wealth takes time. There is no easy button. And that's okay. As they say, easy come...easy go. So if it came in the blink of an eye, it will be gone just as quickly. And you don't want that, do you? You're smarter than that. You care about sustainability. To create a legacy for you and your family. To make in impact far after you're gone.

Now that I've burst that bubble, let's talk about what it really looks like. So while no income is truly passive, there are ways to work smarter. You can put in effort now that is going to pay off tomorrow. Now that's an investment. And investments don't come from nothing. They require capital. They require a buy in.

For example, if you decide you want to build your wealth through investing in rental property, it's going to require effort. You have to have the capital to make the initial investment to purchase a property. You have to pay a broker and an attorney via closing costs. Then you have to handle renovations, which requires either doing the work yourself or finding the right people to do the work for you and then paying them for it. Once all of that is taken care of, you have to market the property. You have to find tenants, whether you are doing short term or long term rentals. Then you have to deal with any service work or breakdowns as they come up.

I think I've made my point. Even "passive" income requires some work. So just decide where you want to put your efforts. Nonetheless, creating additional streams of income is the key to generating true wealth. It also takes diversification into account (more on this later). So if your industry isn't doing well or the market is in a down turn, you have alternative income streams coming in so you can still bring in a solid cash flow to support you and your family.

An additional stream of income might mean generating additional income from rental property like in the example above. It could also mean starting a business. It might mean taking on a side hustle. It could be babysitting, pet sitting, tutoring, you name it. Some people like to resell things online. The options are endless. If you aren't sure where to start, make a list of all of the potential ways you could make money, prioritize them in order of what lights you up the most and then start working your way down the list.

CHAPTER 31

SETTING UP YOUR RATIOS

There are a few things we need to do before we can set up your ratios. Ratios which I like to refer to as:

Save, Spend, & Invest

First, we need to figure out how much you're bringing in and how much is going out in order to establish the above ratios. So to understand how much money you're taking home, do the following exercise:

Write down what you think you make each month. If you know how much you make annually, you can divide that by 12 and remember to take 20-30% out for taxes

Compare to bank statements to ensure this amount is correct

Pro Tip: track it for a month to compare projected vs actual

Understanding how much you spend follows a similar framework:

Write down what you think you spend each month

Compare to bank and credit card statements & any other way you "spend" money IE cash

Pro Tip: track it for a month to compare projected vs actual

Once you have these figures, we can begin setting up your ratios of what you are going to save, spend, & invest.

CHAPTER 32

SAVE

We talked about this a bit above in the sections above. If it's easier for you, stick to one savings account where you keep your cash stronghold. However, if you already have one or you are ready to take your finances to the next level, you can create multiple savings accounts for different purposes.

The first savings account you prioritize should always be the emergency fund or cash stronghold. Once you have funded this account with at least three months of expenses, then you can start focusing on additional savings accounts.

These might include rainy day funds for spontaneous adventures or business opportunities. Another one of my favorites is something I like to call the dream bucket. These funds are for bringing your dreams to life or accomplishing those lofty goals. Maybe that's starting your dream business, retiring early, or traveling the world.

The next thing to think about is what kind of savings account is right for you. What you are using the account for often determines the type of savings account you need. The most important question is probably when are you going to need the funds? On the fly? A few days or a weeks notice? Or is it something you are planning for months or years in advance?

These factors will determine which account is right for you. If you need the money to be accessible in a moments notice, such as for an emergency fund, a traditional savings account with the same financial institution as your checking account is probably the most ideal. You will not be earning any substantial interest, but the money can be transferred to your checking account instantly.

On the other hand, if you are okay with waiting a few days up to a week, then I recommend getting a money market account. These accounts typically offer interest rates between 1.5-3%, which can be up to 150 to 300 times greater than interest rates on traditional savings accounts such as Chase. **Read that again.** You may have to put in a request for the funds which can either be transferred electronically or mailed to you in a check and this will usually take between 3-5 business days. If you ask me, I'd say WORTH IT.

I use All American Bank for my MM account (MM = money market, might as well start to get comfortable with the lingo finance professionals are using) which offers a rate of 1.5%. This was one of the highest yields on the market when I set up the account a couple of years ago. Now Goldman Sachs and other financial institutions have rates upwards of 3%.

There are also CDs and other short term investment vehicles that can be used as a savings account. CDs, or certificate of deposit, are among the safest investments available from banks and credit unions. They typically pay higher interest rates than savings accounts and money market accounts, but there's one key difference. You have to tie your money up in the account for a specified period of time. It's possible to get out early, but you'll most likely pay a penalty.

How it works is that the financial institution offers an interest rate premium in exchange for the customer agreeing to leave a lump-sum deposit untouched for a predetermined period of time, such as 6, 12, or 18 months for example. Almost all consumer financial institutions offer them, although shopping around is crucial to finding the best CD rates because different financial institutions offer a surprisingly wide range. Your traditional brick and mortar bank might pay an extremely low rate on even long-term CDs, for example, while an online bank or local credit union might pay three to five times the national average.

CDs, being part savings account and part investment, are only the tip of the iceberg. There is so much more information I am excited to share with you regarding investments. The ways to make your money work for you are endless! So stay tuned for that.

CHAPTER 33

SPEND

There's a reason I tell you to think about how much you want to pay yourself and how much you want to save FIRST. That's because if we put spending first, most of us would spend everything we had and there would be nothing left. For many of you, living paycheck to paycheck may be your current reality. So now that you know how much you want to pay yourself and how much you want to save, let's talk about how much you spend.

GET LEAN. What things can you cut out completely or live without? Reduce? Reuse? Make last longer? We can't create sustainable wealth if we are living wasteful lives as unconscious consumers. Remember, today's sacrifice is tomorrow's reward. Now I don't support or condone sacrificing things that you legitimately need or neglecting yourself past the point of reason. You need to take care of you. And stressing yourself out majorly just to save a couple of extra bucks isn't the answer. The biggest factor in your overall financial situation is your earning power. So don't cut yourself off at the knees from ignoring your basic needs and further diminish your earning potential by neglecting your health. You feel me?

However, most Americans are spending way more than they make. They are buying things that they don't need and can't even afford, just because they are trying to keep up with the Kardashians (or the Jones' depending on your era). We as a collective have quite literally racked up trillions of dollars of debt, more than we can even repay in our lifetime. Which means we are leaving our children and our grandchildren to pick up the pieces.

So let's shift that paradigm. Let's break the cycle of debt and financial overwhelm once and for all. This means talking about money. With our peers, with our partners, and with our children. Let's destigmatize and open the dialogue around finances. So that rather than avoiding them or feeling like they are in the dark, the next generation can make empowered choices around their finances. They can start out on the right foot with a solid foundation rather than spending years paying for their mistakes. Let's leave the world even better off than the way we found it. That ideology, sometimes referred to as the campground principle, is at the core of true sustainability.

If you have excessive amounts of debt, start to make a plan to pay it off. Depending on your interest rates, you may want to pay off debt before you start building out additional savings funds. I personally feel more comfortable establishing a cash stronghold first, then focusing on paying down debt in a 70/30 allocation. Meaning that 70% of what I'm setting aside goes towards investments and 30% goes towards paying down debt. My husband on the other hand employed an inverse allocation of 30/70 when we were saving to purchase our first home as he had more debt. More on paying down debt in the section about investments and compound interest included below.

CHAPTER 34

BUDGET: GETTING A HANDLE ON INCOME & EXPENSES

Now that you have an idea of what you're spending and what you can cut out, let's formalize it in a budget. For those of you that just cringed at the sound of that word, let me set you free. There's a reason I waited until you had a good idea of what your money situation is looking like before I dropped the "B" word. By the time we're done, my goal is that you no longer see "budget as a dirty word. And for the really savvy women, you may even start to LOVE it.

You've heard of the saying you've got to say no to say yes, right? Well, money isn't any different. Every time you say no to frivolous spending, you are saying yes to your dreams. Every time you say no to wasting money, you are saying yes to your legacy. For you and for your family. You are saying yes to starting that business, putting your children through school, retiring your parents, or whatever it is that you're called to do. You feel me?

We'll cover the basics of budgeting here. However, if you need additional support or want to dive deeper into this, feel free to check out my complimentary budgeting resources at www.budgetspreadsheets.healmoneytrauma.com/home321 74136. This includes free sheets for budgeting, tracking your spending, a calendar to note important dates or autopayments, and a debt payoff tracker. I highly recommend you use them or another resource to hold you accountable, keep you organized, and make it fun! I like to print out these sheets and break out all of my colorful gel pens when my husband and I budget each month.

Believe it or not, you've already done most of the work. Yay! **happy dance** You've already determined how much you make per month, you've determined how much you're spending, and you've determined how much you want to save. So now we just have to bring it all together! Either using the budget sheets I provided as a resource above or on your own spreadsheet, go ahead and write all of this down.

There are a few different kinds of budgeting. Zero-based budget, the envelope system aka cash budgeting, reverse budgeting, & Balanced Money Formula to name a few. We will be using a hybrid of a few of these here, as that's what works best for me. So feel free to tweak this and use whatever system works best for you.

Step 1: Start with income at the top.

Step 2: Take out the pay yourself first amount. The remaining value is your gross income.

Step 3: From gross income, subtract your expenses.

Pro tip: I recommend splitting your expenses up into categories such as groceries, utilities, rent/mortgage, etc.

Step 4: Calculate your Net Income (Income - Savings - Expenses = NI).

Step 5: Whatever funds are left over, this is money you have to play with in investments or an additional savings account.

CHAPTER 35

INVEST

Money, just like energy, shouldn't just be stored for no reason. You should have the amount you need to feel secure and prepare for an emergency, as discussed above under the cash stronghold section. But not so much that you start to become a hoarder and take on the appearance of a crazy cat lady. If you don't have your money working for you, your money will be sitting around collecting dust. And in turn that means your money, and your dreams, will never be able to reach their full potential.

Let's look at the stats. Women earning $50K a year in their 20s & 30s has anywhere from $400,000-$1,000,000 in lifetime losses compared to men due to lack of investing.[x] Say whatttt? & if you're older than that, the numbers are slightly lower. But still! We are talking some serious cash. So what are we gonna do about it, ladies? I say it's about time we rally together and get our money working for us!

Before we dive into all the different kinds of investments, there are a few things to think about. First of all, what is your risk appetite? Determine which of the following best describes you:

Risk taker - high risk appetite, usually applies to those at a younger age.

Risk neutral - moderate risk appetite, usually applies during middle age.

Risk averse - low risk appetite, usually makes the most sense during older age near or during retirement.

The next question to ask yourself is what are your financial goals? Are you saving for a home? Starting a business? Saving for retirement? Are you trying to maintain wealth?

Build wealth? All of this is going to determine the kind of investments you are going to make. For example, the duration of the investments you are looking for IE whether they are short term (ST) or long term (LT), etc. If you need help figuring out what your financial goals are, I'd love to help. Reach out to me directly or hop in the FB group for additional support:

https://www.facebook.com/groups/henryettas/

The next thing to think about is how much capital you have to work with. After doing the exercises above, you should have an idea of how much capital, or funds, you have to put towards an investment. If you are still unclear and would like additional support, check out my free 3 Step Guide to Manifesting Wealth www.manifestingwealth.healmoneytrauma.com. This will help you get an even better idea of where you're at & where you want to go.

Common misconception: you have to have a ton of money to start investing. You don't. But it will determine HOW you start to invest. Lots of mutual funds have a minimum, such as $5k or $10k. In addition, certain financial advisors have a minimum portfolio size that they will work with. If you have that & you are ready to get serious, then I highly recommend hiring a financial advisor to manage your wealth. This is what the pros do. This is what the 1% are doing. & there's no reason you shouldn't be doing it too. More on this in the next section.

However, if you aren't quite there yet, there are alternative options. ETFs are a great place to start, which I will describe below. There are also apps such as Stash & Robinhood to help make investing easier and more accessible which I share more about in the resource portion following this strategy section.

DIFFERENT KINDS OF INVESTMENTS

Stocks - Also known as shares in a corporation or equity, stocks are a type of security that signal proportionate ownership in the issuing company. Corporations issue stocks in order to raise capital for operation or expansion. Bought and sold mostly on stock exchanges, while there can be private sales as well, stocks are the foundation of almost every portfolio. These transactions have to follow compliance and government regulations which are meant to protect investors from fraud. It is also worth noting that stock prices are driven by expectations of corporate earnings or profits.

Bonds - A bond is a fixed income vehicle that represents a loan made by an investor to a borrower, usually corporate or governmental. Bond details include the end date when the principal of the loan is due to be paid to the bond owner and typically include the terms for variable or fixed interest payments made by the borrower. U.S. Govt bonds for example is one of the safest investments you can make, because they have never defaulted on a bond. As is to be expected though, less risk means a lower return.

Mutual Funds - Investments that pool your money together with other investors to purchase shares of a combination of stocks, bonds, or other securities, referred to as a portfolio, that might be difficult to acquire on your own. They are usually overseen by a fund manager and often have a minimum buy in. There are some options out there nowadays with buy ins as low as $100, however most are a few thousand. It is also worth noting that due to the fund being actively managed by someone else, the fees are often higher for mutual funds compared to other investments.

Index Funds - Index funds are mutual funds that are designed to track the returns of a market index. An index is a group of securities that represents a particular segment of the market. This could be the stock market, the bond market, etc. Some of the most well-known companies that develop market indexes are Standard & Poors and Dow Jones. You've likely heard of at least one of these at some point or another, be it on the news or during your own research. In addition, index funds are generally considered ideal core portfolio holdings for retirement accounts.

ETFs - Exchange-traded funds that are a collection of securities, such as stocks, that track an underlying index. For example, the S&P 500. S&P stands for Standard and Poor, the names of the two founding financial companies and it's a compilation of the stocks of the 500 largest U.S. companies. It represents the stock market's performance by reporting the risks and returns of the biggest companies.

fund and an ETF are similar, there are

ices. ETFs can be traded more easily than

and traditional mutual funds, similar to how

commo. stocks are traded on a stock exchange. There is

also less of a barrier to entry as investors can also buy

ETFs in smaller sizes than mutual funds. Mutual funds and

thus index funds are also priced at the end of the day,

whereas ETFs can be traded throughout the day like a

normal stock.

Alternative Investments - Of course you can also invest
directly in someone else's business that you know
personally or professionally. You can invest in real estate.
You can invest in commodities and derivatives. However,
many of these are a bit higher level and are rarely discussed
in association with those who are just starting out in
investing. If you are interested in learning more about these
kinds of investments, I highly recommend doing some
research or speaking to a financial advisor.

Something important to note about all of the investment
vehicles mentioned above is that they are designed to buy
and hold, in other words they are long term strategies.

Looking at the way the market is performing on a given day or even a given year is a sure way to worry yourself into a frenzy. Long term investments are better understood when you look at long term performance of at least 3-5 years.

Retirement

As our life expectancy grows, the need for a solid retirement plan becomes increasingly important. A lot of people also talk about wanting to retire early. This requires enough savings, investment income, or pension income to cover your living expenses. Once you have achieved this, work becomes optional.

In order to have enough money set aside to stop working around the standard retirement age of 65, you have to start early. Either you have to start saving young, say in your 20's and 30's, saving at least 10% of your income each year, or start saving late, say in your 40's and 50's, setting aside a large portion of your income at as much as 50% a year. I don't know about you, but 10% sounds a lot better to me than 50%. Plus, if you decide to build a family and have kids, 40-50+ might be the time when your children are going to college and you incur additional expenses as a result of the rapidly growing secondary education costs. So play smarter and set yourself up for success now. Your future self will thank you.

There are also numerous benefits of retirement accounts as an investment vehicle. This includes tax advantages such as deferment and reducing your annual taxable income, which in turn decreases your present tax liability. This is the main reason why many people utilize their retirement account for a large portion of their investments. However, if you are investing for something more short term, you may want to seek alternative investment vehicles as there are often large penalties for early withdrawals from retirement accounts. The nuances vary with each type of retirement account, which are described below.

401(k) Plans - A 401(k) plan is a retirement account that's offered as an employee benefit. It allows you to contribute a portion of your pre-tax paycheck to tax-deferred investments. This reduces your taxable income, IE you incur less taxes in a given year. Investment gains grow tax deferred until you withdraw the money in retirement. Many plans also offer the opportunity to borrow against the funds in the form of a loan.

You should also find out if your employer matches your contributions, and if so you want to do your best to max that out. Be sure to ask if they have a vesting period, which is a prescribed period of time you must stay with your employer before you have full ownership of their contributions to your 401(k). This period of time can vary by company, so it's worth checking with your individual employer. To clarify, all the money that you personally contributed to your 401(k) is yours and will go with you if you choose to leave your job. Something else to take into consideration is that investment choices for these types of plans are often limited, and management and administrative fees can be high. The IRS also imposes contribution limits per year, although limits for 401(k) plans are more generous than those for other plans: $19,000 in 2019, up from $18,500 in 2018. This increases to $25,000 if you're age 50 or older.

IRAs - Individual retirement accounts, or IRAs, are investment accounts with tax benefits. You can use the account to invest in stocks, bonds, mutual funds, ETFs, and other types of investments after you place money into it. You can also make the investment decisions yourself or hire someone else to do it for you. You might consider investing in an IRA if your employer doesn't offer a retirement plan or you can also use this as a secondary account if you've maxed out your 401(k) contributions for the year. You can contribute up to $6,000 in 2019 and increases to $7,000 if you're age 50 or older. You'll pay no taxes annually on investment gains, which allows them to grow more quickly. Many taxpayers can even deduct their IRA contributions on their income tax returns if they don't also have a 401(k) retirement account at work, reducing their taxable income for that year.

Roth IRAs - Unlike a traditional IRA, Roth IRA contributions are made with after-tax dollars. However, any money generated within the Roth is never taxed again. You can also withdraw contributions you've made to them before retirement age without penalty once five years have passed since your first contribution. Another benefit is you're not required to begin taking withdrawals at age 70 as you are with traditional IRAs, 401(k)s, and other retirement savings plans. Putting money in a Roth is a great place to invest extra cash if you're just starting out and you think your income will grow.

Roth 401(k) - combines features of the Roth IRA and a 401(k). It's a type of account offered through employers, and it's relatively new. As with a Roth IRA, contributions come from your paycheck after-tax and contributions and earnings are never taxed again if you remain in the plan for at least five years. However, there is a caveat with this type of plan. Contribution limits become stricter if your modified adjusted gross income (MAGI) reaches a certain point, until contributions are prohibited entirely if you earn too much. Phaseouts begin at MAGIs of $122,000 for single filers in 2019, and you can't contribute if your MAGI tops $137,000. These limits for married taxpayers filing joint returns increase to $193.000 and $203,000.

Simple IRA - SIMPLE IRA stands for Savings Incentive Match for Employees and is a retirement plan that small businesses with up to 100 employees can offer. It works very much like a 401(k). Contributions are made with pretax paycheck withdrawals, and the money grows tax deferred until retirement. However, you can't borrow from a SIMPLE IRA the way you can from a 401(k).

SEP IRA - This is specifically for those who are self-employed with no employees. It allows you to contribute a portion of your income to your own retirement account and you can fully deduct these contributions from your taxable income. The maximum annual contribution limits are higher than most other retirement accounts with tax advantages: $56,000 or 25% of income, whichever is less, as of 2019.

CHAPTER 36

COMPOUND INTEREST

Often called the eighth wonder of the world, understanding compound interest is instrumental to your financial success. It is said in the financial industry that you will either be making it or paying it. If you're reading this book, I take it you know which side of the equation you'd rather be on and you are ready to start making it!

So what the heck is it? Compound interest is the addition of interest to the principal sum of a loan or deposit. In other words, it is interest on interest. From the side of the grantor or lender (which if you are investing, is YOU), this is AMAZING. However, from the side of the debtor or borrower (IE tons of credit card debt or excessive loans) this can be extremely detrimental, causing numerous problems over time.

The table below illustrates a few simple examples of compound interest. We are looking at this mostly from the perspective of the investor.

	Growth of $100	Compounded Annual Return
Scenario 1	$161.05	10%
Scenario 2	$156.82	9%
Scenario 3	$120.12	4%
Scenario 4	$31.82	-20%

However, if you are curious about what this would mean as a debtor, imagine this: you have spent $100 on a loan or credit at an interest rate of 10%. After one year, that $100 will actually end up costing you $161.05. So you can imagine what 30K of credit card debt could cost you. And it just goes up every year. Yikes!

Important Note About Debt

If you have debt, don't panic. Just make a plan. Make a plan to start paying it down before you start to focus all of your attention on investing. I prefer to operate from the standard that if your debt is at an interest rate of 3-5% or lower, invest your money over paying it down. I like to call this "healthy debt." This is because, depending on your investment strategy, you will likely be making more from your investments than holding the debt is costing you.

However, if you are holding debt at a rate higher than 5% (IE any credit card in existence) than use the money you're setting aside to invest to pay down these balances first. I'd recommend prioritizing credit cards and debt with the highest interest rates first. You should be able to find the rates on your statements, otherwise call the lender and ask.

I'd also like to share an empowering mindset shift to employ if you are feeling overwhelmed about your debt. Rather than seeing it as a burden, realize that someone trusted you to pay them back. They trusted you and found you credible enough to extend you this line of credit. Another awesome reframing is considering your debt a record of blessings already received.

CHAPTER 37

INVESTING IN THE SUPPORT YOU NEED

Let's be honest, the stuff we're getting into is pretty detailed and this is only a brief snapshot. Everyone's financial situation is different, your goals are different, and you deserve a unique approach to your unique situation. A financial advisor can help you create a roadmap to where you would like to go.

Think about it this way: if you were training to compete in the Olympics, would you hire a coach? Definitely. So why treat your finances and your life any differently? Your financial life can be like a marathon with consciously chosen & vetted advisors cheering you on and helping you along the way, or it can be like a grueling obstacle course where you get knocked down in the mud face first over and over again. Some of you might be into that sort of thing, but I personally would choose the former.

My financial advisors are Zak and Marc of I.M. Financial. They run a family business, which aligns strongly with my husband and I's values. Zak is also a good friend who takes pride in educating his clients about the wealth building process. He shares information that the big banks don't want you to know so you can utilize the best strategies to grow your portfolio. He is also a strong advocate for women and makes a conscious effort to make room for women at every table. They advise not only my husband and I, but also the rest of my family. This has been incredibly beneficial in coming together as a unit to build our legacy and work together with complete synergy.

I'd also like to add that investing in the support you need goes beyond finding the right financial advisor. There are many key people that will help you on your journey to creating sustainable wealth, and having a team that works together seamlessly will save you a ton of time, energy, and money. These people could include an accountant such as tax professional, an attorney for estate planning, and even a coach to assist you with mindset, strategy and provide accountability. Ensure that your vision and goals are communicated consistently to all parties and that they are working together to provide a plan that works for you. I actually like to go as far as introducing these people so that they can take ownership of quarterbacking information to each other so you are not playing phone tag and being the middle man.

How do you know when it's the right time to hire a coach? Well, you can do it proactively if you're smarter than me…orrr you can wait until you hit your breaking point and everything is falling apart. It's up to you. When I was toiling away as an accountant making about 60K a year, overworking, and running a biz that made me miserable, something finally occurred to me. After trying to balance happiness and becoming wildly profitable & being unsuccessful at it on my own, perhaps it would be wise to get some help. This is when I made the commitment to hire my first coach.

Her energy was incredible. She came recommended from people I trusted. I knew she had mastered what I wanted to be doing, and had built the kind of business for herself that I wanted to have. In order to afford the investment, I needed to max out my credit card and even pull out of our investment accounts to make the BIGGEST INVESTMENT I HAD EVER MADE IN MY LIFE.

$6,000 and a whole lot of tears later, I called her and gave her my credit card number. I made the first payment and thought, oh shit. Where is this money going to come from? Honestly, I didn't know and I didn't care. Not because I'm irresponsible, but because I fully trusted myself to do whatever the hell it took to make this possible. And to show up, put in the work, and transform my life and business.

Some people may consider the decision I made irresponsible. It was a few months after quit my cushy corporate job. I was a newlywed and new homeowner, with a whole new set of responsibilities...including a mortgage in one of the most expensive areas in the United States. All of the evidence said no. It was impractical and nonsensical. However, I believed in the unseen. I believed in my potential and I believed in my dreams. I knew deep down inside there was a better way.

And guess what? It was the best decision I ever made in my business. Hands down. If I hadn't taken a leap of faith, I very well could be writing a book on burnout instead of creating sustainable wealth.

When I hired my first coach, I made a commitment to do the work. I showed up. I stretched myself outside of my comfort zone. I did the work. I went deep and faced every fear that had ever held me back, from fear of failure to perfectionism and everything in between. I had so many crucial conversations I can't even count and created boundaries that empowered me to build my dream business.

And the results showed. I showed up for myself & my clients like never before. I went from a former Corporate Accountant and running a business doing the same blasé work to a Money Consciousness Coach, a best-selling Author, & a leading expert in my industry.

Doing things I LOVE and working with women who light me up & inspire me to show up powerfully for them every damn day! Helping them to feel confident and powerful through owning their personal & business finances. Creating a plan to generate consistent high level income in their businesses, pay down debt, and build a legacy for themselves & their families.

What if I told you this is completely possible for you too? That you can get paid to do what you love, build sustainable wealth, and manifest your wildest dreams! Would it be worth maxing out your credit card for? Would it be worth calling up that family member you don't really like to ask for the cash? Would it be worth taking that side job to invest in building a fabulous life beyond anything you could even imagine?

I was overworked, unappreciated, and miserable. I dreaded doing client work, clocking my hours, chasing down payments. Every day felt like a struggle of forcing myself out of bed and talking myself into doing the things I had to do. I would constantly think to myself, this isn't what I quit my 9-5 for.

My business was running me instead of me running my business. And I did the work because I "had" to, not because I wanted to. I did it because it paid the bills and, as a responsible adult, that was important to me.

But you know what's more important? Your soul. Doing work that lights you up and sparks a fire inside of you. One that grows and spreads, allowing you to share the light with others. Jumping out of bed excited for what the day brings! Feeling good about what you're doing and having a massive impact.

There is no amount of money that can buy happiness. Sure, it can make life a bit more convenient. It may even afford you a few luxuries that will make you feel good, for a while. But it can't buy fulfillment. So what is it that lights you up?

What is it that sets your heart on fire and turns you into a ray of sunshine while rainbows dance around your head?

Do that. Do that thing. Invest in that. Spend the time, hire that coach, find the money, do whatever the hell it takes. Because life is too short to settle for mediocrity. You only get one shot at this thing, so you might as well make it worth it.

You are a f*cking miracle. Walking, living proof that life is beautiful, intentional, and that miracles can happen. All you have to do is make a choice. A choice to believe and to do whatever it takes to make it happen. This faith combined with some good ole hard work (work ethic) will align everything else you need in your favor.

I should also mention something. Don't be surprised if it doesn't manifest in exactly the way you imagined. Be open to the universe providing & showing up for you in unexpected ways. Open to receiving infinite blessings from God. They are always working in your favor.

CHAPTER 38

IMPORTANT THINGS TO NOTE

TAXES

Interest, dividends, & realized capital gains are a few things to be aware of regarding taxation. So for example if you are seeking to raise $50K for a down payment on a home, you need to ensure you are planning with your advisor to generate $50K after tax as opposed to $50K in returns. Make sense? Either way, I highly recommend consulting a tax professional in addition to bringing this to your advisors attention so you are fully aware of the tax ramifications of your investing strategies.

FINANCIAL GOALS & TIMING

The financial goals you have are different than the financial goals I have. And that's one of the few reasons the two investment strategies might differ. One thing to take into consideration is whether your financial goals are short term (ST) or long term (LT). Starting a business or purchasing a home such as the example above may be considerably shorter term than say, saving for retirement. Thus the strategies for each might differ. This is another element to take into consideration as you are mapping out your investment strategy and something your financial advisor will take into consideration when building your financial plan.

RISK APPETITE

This refers to your willingness to take on risk. As a precursor, risk has a direct relationship with return. If you take on more risk, there should be a higher chance of return. Thus if you take on less risk, there is likely a lower chance of return. So someone that has a high risk appetite is willing to take on more risk. Someone that has a moderate risk appetite would be more neutral to risk. And someone that has a low risk appetite is generally more averse to taking on risks. If you are not sure where you fall on the spectrum, using your age is a good place to start. One method suggests to start with the number 100. Then subtract your age from that number, and the remaining number is the percentage of your portfolio that you should be investing in something like growth stocks which are typically considered riskier investments. IE if you are 35 then 100-35=65. So 65% of your investments should be a bit riskier such as growth stocks, while 35% of your investments should be more risk averse or secure such as bonds & utilities.

HOW MUCH MONEY YOU'LL BE INVESTING

Often referred to as a "nest egg," this is the amount of money you have to start (or continue) investing with. This is not to be confused with contributions, which is the money you will be continuing to add to your portfolio on a weekly, monthly, or annual basis. This nest egg will determine the type of investments that are available to you. This is because numerous investments require minimums, such as 5K, 10K, or even more. Don't let this discourage you, there are plenty of investment platforms such as Ellevest, Stash, & Robinhood that don't require a minimum. Even Vanguard and E-Trade offer certain options without minimums. I also don't recommend seeking a financial advisor to manage your portfolio until you are working with a nest egg of 10K or more. The time and energy it takes to find the right fit and the fees associated with it typically don't balance out until you're at this point. However, that doesn't mean you can't get started or be smart about saving & investing. If anything, I'd say it's all the more reason! Set a goal for yourself and as you get closer to reaching that goal, start to make a few appointments with financial advisors so you can find the right fit for when you're ready.

DIVERSIFICATION

This is a risk management strategy that mixes a wide variety of investments within a portfolio. The reason for this is to mitigate nonsystematic risk, which is uncertainty inherent to a specific company or industry. Examples of this include industry performance, shifts in management, regulatory changes, employee strikes, or lawsuits against a company to name a few. This is a necessary element to introduce to any solid investment portfolio and something a financial advisor will take into account as they put together your portfolio.

CHAPTER 39

ADDITIONAL RESOURCES

1. My financial advisors – Izak and Marc of IM Financial www.im-financial.com

2. **Apps for budgeting & saving**
   a. Mint - budgeting, saving app. You can also view all of your accounts in one place.
   b. Ally - if you want an online banking platform where you can create multiple accounts at no additional cost.

3. **Apps & platforms for investing**
   a. Stash - ETFs & you can also choose funds that align with your interests & values. You can start investing with as little as $5.
   b. Robinhood - Individual stocks that are commission free with no minimums. I prefer Robinhood because the fees are lower, however I've used both & they are a great place to start. Once you have a few grand put aside, I would recommend looking for a financial advisor to assist you in managing your portfolio.
   c. Ellevest - Investing platform for women by women, Founded by Sallie Krawcheck of Wall Street.

4. **Resources for freelancers**
   a. Trupo - Benefits packages & insurance for freelancers, because entrepreneurs deserve to have a safety net too. Includes options such as dental, accident, & specified disease insurance. www.trupo.com/partners/lawless?utm_sourc e=lawless

5. I put together a few complimentary financial resources to support your journey. Feel free to download one or all of them below:

- 3 Step Guide to Manifesting Wealth
  http://manifestingwealth.healmoneytrauma.com
- Budget Sheets
  http://budgetspreadsheets.healmoneytrauma.com/home32174136
- Guided Meditation: Manifest Wealth & Prosperity
  http://wealthmeditation.healmoneytrauma.com/home32175802

ACKNOWLEDGEMENTS

Thank you to every single one of you who picked up this book. You are an agent for change and I want to honor you for courageously taking a bold step to help awaken and transform the consciousness of the planet. To shift the dialogue around money, something engrained so deeply in our society, is no easy feat.

I'd also like to give a huge thank you to my Editor & Publishing Coach Liz Lawless, whom I'm lucky enough to call my Aunt, for her countless hours of support and incredible strategies. Thank you to my team, especially my Executive Assistant Alyssa Watson Lee who held me accountable to my deadlines and spearheaded all of the tech implementation as well as cover art for the book. I would also like to thank my best friend and amazing photographer Tanner Albright for his work on the cover and his illustrations found throughout the book. A huge thanks to all of the phenomenal women who vulnerably shared their transformational stories so that other women could learn and grow from them. Lysa, Valeria, Allie, Angel, & Kiele, I love you all! And an additional thank you to my mother Lysa Lawless for always believing in me and telling me I could do anything - including become a best selling author. Your strength and desire to grow & build a legacy for our family inspire me every day.

I would also like to give some serious honor and appreciation to my incredible husband Jesse Borcina who has been by my side for countless early mornings & late nights as this book was birthed into the world. Thank you for speaking life into me and always supporting me while I make my wildest dreams a reality. You da bae. I'd also like to mention my coaches Louiza and Rachel Luna, as well as all of the Expansion & Activated Mastermind girls. Your support, accountability, and insight has meant the world to me over this past year. Thank you to all of my friends and family too that didn't get annoyed with my limited availability and supported my vision. Y'all are awesome! And thank you to the leadership at V1 Church as well as the Dream Team who declare greatness over my life every week and share my vision of honoring God through relationship over religion. It's an honor to lovingly support people from broken to breakthrough and from breakthrough to triumph with you all.

REFERENCES

i "Webster's Dictionary" WWWebster Dictionary: WWW Dictionary, Merriam-Webster, Inc., 1999.

ii Rebecca Gladding, M.D. "This Is Your Brain on Meditation." Psychology Today, Sussex Publishers, www.psychologytoday.com/us/blog/use-your-mind-change-your-brain/201305/is-your-brain-meditation

iii Emma Seppälä M.D. "20 Scientific Reasons to Start Meditating Today." Psychology Today, Sussex Publishers, www.psychologytoday.com/us/blog/feeling-it/201309/20-scientific-reasons-start-meditating-today

iv "Which Type of Meditation Style Is Best For You?" Gaia, www.gaia.com/article/which-type-meditation-style-best-for-you

v Noma Nazish. "Five Reasons To Keep A Journal In 2018." Forbes, Forbes Magazine, 10 Jan. 2018, www.forbes.com/sites/nomanazish/2017/12/29/five-legit-reasons-to-keep-a-journal-in-2018/#2cb27d3155e1

vi Steven Pressfield, *The War of Art: Break through the Blocks and Win Your Inner Creative Battles.* Black Irish Entertainment LLC, 2012.

vii Eckhart Tolle. *The Power of Now.* Hachette Australia, 2018.

233

[viii] Quotes #1-6 credits of Sallie Krawcheck, Founder of Ellevest, an investing platform for women.

[ix] Quotes #7-8 credits of Valentina Zarya, "Venture Capital's Funding Gender Gap Is Actually Getting Worse," Fortune, March 13, 2017, http://fortune.com/2017/03/13/female-founders-venture-capital

[x] Sallie Krawcheck, Founder of Ellevest, an investing platform for women.